Basilea Schlink

PATMOS
When the Heavens Opened

LAKELAND
MARSHALL, MORGAN & SCOTT
116 Baker Street, London W1M 2BB

First British Edition – 1976

ISBN 0 551 00756 7

Cover photo: scene on the island of Patmos in late summer 1975

Printed in Great Britain by
Hunt Barnard Printing Ltd, Aylesbury, Bucks

Contents

The revelation of Jesus Christ, which God gave him to show to his servants what must soon take place; and he made it known by sending his angel to his servant John, who bore witness to the word of God and to the testimony of Jesus Christ, even to all that he saw. Blessed is he who reads aloud the words of the prophecy, and blessed are those who hear, and who keep what is written therein; for the time is near.

John to the seven churches that are in Asia:

Grace to you and peace from him who is and who was and who is to come, and from the seven spirits who are before his throne, and from Jesus Christ the faithful witness, the first-born of the dead, and the ruler of kings on earth.

To him who loves us and has freed us from our sins by his blood and made us a kingdom, priests to his God and Father, to him be glory and dominion for ever and ever. Amen. Behold, he is coming with the clouds, and every eye will see him, every one who pierced him; and all tribes of the earth will wail on account of him. Even so. Amen.

"I am the Alpha and the Omega," says the Lord God, who is and who was and who is to come, the Almighty.

I John, your brother, who share with you in Jesus the tribulation and the kingdom and the patient endurance, was on the island called Patmos on account of the word of God and the testimony of Jesus. I was in the Spirit on the Lord's day, and I heard behind me a loud voice like a trumpet saying, "Write what you see in a book and send it to the seven churches, to Ephesus and to Smyrna and to Pergamum and to Thyatira and to Sardis and to Philadelphia and to Laodicea."

Then I turned to see the voice that was speaking to me, and on turning I saw seven golden lampstands, and in the midst of the lampstands one like a son of man, clothed with a long robe and with a golden girdle round his breast, his head and his hair were white as white wool, white as snow; his eyes were like a flame of fire, his feet were like burnished bronze, refined as in a furnace, and his voice was like the sound of many waters; in his right hand he held seven stars, from his mouth issued a sharp two-edged sword, and his face was like the sun shining in full strength.

When I saw him, I fell at his feet as though dead. But he laid his right hand upon me, saying, "Fear not, I am the first and the last, and the living one; I died, and behold I am alive for evermore, and I have the keys of Death and Hades. Now write what you see, what is and what is to take place hereafter."   Revelation 1:1-19

A Personal Word of Introduction

The Lord had prepared a special gift for me in late summer 1975 — a visit to the island of Patmos. Friends had offered me a small house there, where I could come apart for a time of prayer in solitude. And so it happened that I was privileged to spend a few weeks on the island of Patmos, where the Apostle John lived in exile — most likely from AD 95–97. In Revelation 1 he says, "I was on the island called Patmos on account of the word of God and the testimony of Jesus." Because of his testimony to Jesus, he was banished when the Christians were persecuted. This meant great suffering for him, as is evident from his words, "I John, who also am your brother, and companion in tribulation, and in the kingdom and patience of Jesus Christ" (Revelation 1:9 AV).

Often I would climb up the steep donkey path leading to the grotto, which since the first centuries of Christianity has been recognized as the historical site where the Apostle John received the Revelation of Jesus Christ. The events of long ago are still captured in the atmosphere of the grotto. Upon entering, I could immediately sense the presence of God. It was like being in a holy temple, and I was constrained to kneel down at this site, where not only the Apostle John, the favourite disciple of Jesus, had set foot, but where Jesus Himself had appeared and imparted an awe-inspiring revelation.

In the past I had visited many places that were of significance for the Kingdom of God and I had been blessed by the great deeds God had performed there in the lives of godly men long ago. But at this holy site my heart trembled, overwhelmed by the awe-inspiring event that had taken place here.

In a small book that I read about Patmos the following thoughts were expressed. Once before, the Son of

God had descended to a grotto. That was in Bethlehem, where He descended as the incarnate Word of God, a little Child. The grotto in the land of Israel heard the first cries of the newborn Son of God and Son of man. And here on this small, insignificant island there was another grotto. But this time the Son of God, the Lord and King, Jesus Christ, appeared in all His majesty and splendour. Whereas in Bethlehem the Most High descended humbly with His sovereignty veiled, here on the island of Patmos the Lord appeared in His power and glory. And I could sense His majesty as I tarried in prayer at this site, often for many hours alone.

Tradition still marks the place where John fell to the ground like a dead man at the appearance of Jesus in His majesty and power as Judge, and today it is enclosed by a grating. An icon depicting the event can be found above the historic spot. Contemplating this picture, I read the passage in Revelation where John writes: "On turning I saw seven golden lampstands, and in the midst of the lampstands one like a son of man, clothed with a long robe and with a golden girdle round his breast; his head and his hair were white as white wool, white as snow; his eyes were like a flame of fire, his feet were like burnished bronze, refined as in a furnace, and his voice was like the sound of many waters" (Revelation 1:12 b-15).

I could understand why John fell to the ground like a dead man. As Jesus' favourite disciple had he not been very close to Him? Had not Jesus inclined Himself to him and revealed His heart to him like a friend to a friend? And had not John heard gracious words of love from his Master's lips? But it was a different Jesus that now stood before him. His voice was powerful, like the sound of many waters. His eyes were like a flame of fire, deeply earnest and filled with holy wrath. And His feet were strong and firm like solid bronze. The majesty of

Jesus cast John to the ground – he was unable to remain on his feet. And then came the voice commanding him, "Write!"

John was to write down the Apocalypse, the mighty Revelation of Jesus, which speaks of the age of God's wrath. But he could not convey to others the message of God's holy wrath and His great judgments unless he himself had first seen Jesus in His sovereignty and might as Judge. Nor could he write that in the end times people would be terror-stricken to behold His wrath-filled countenance, unless he himself had experienced this fear as he beheld Jesus as the wrathful Lord and Judge. He could proclaim only that which he had personally experienced.

Jesus was able to disclose to John the great affliction of the believers in the end times, only because John had personally undergone a long period of hardship and was enduring deep suffering here in Patmos. He was the only one of the Eleven not to die a martyr's death. After the others had gone, he alone was left. According to ancient tradition, before the exile in Patmos, John had made his home in Ephesus with the Mother Mary, for upon the cross Jesus had given her to John as his mother and chosen him to be her son. Then she too was called to her heavenly home and again John was left behind. Many years passed by and still he was not permitted to enter the heavenly glory to be with his Lord, whom he dearly loved. Finally when he was an old man, probably in his nineties, persecution broke out under the Emperor Domitian. Many of the brethren were called home to the Lord, and once again John had to remain behind. Moreover, he was banished to a rugged, pagan island, where he was a stranger and an outcast. This is why he writes to the churches in affliction, saying that he is their brother and companion in suffering and patient endurance.

Now as the fruit of his suffering John receives the Apocalypse – the revelation that had been given by God to Jesus Christ. He is permitted to hear his Master's voice again – a mighty voice and yet so kind. "Fear not, I [your Master, whom you know and who loves you] am the first and the last, and the living one" (Revelation 1:17 f.).

During those weeks, especially when I was praying in the grotto, the Apostle John came alive for me in all his suffering, but also in his experience of the immeasurable love and anguished wrath of his Lord and Master, Jesus Christ. How moved I was at the thought that Jesus should give John a vision of the mighty end-battle between heaven and hell, light and darkness, and reveal to him the hidden plans of God! Equally so I was filled with awe that Jesus should let His disciple John see the glory He has prepared for those who love Him, and that He should let him behold the consummation of all God's ways and leadings.

What a privilege it was to be here! As I prayed in the grotto, I was constrained to worship the Lord, because the prophecy made known to John here almost 2,000 years ago is beginning to be fulfilled today and is becoming a reality before our eyes. To be at this very place at this point in history was a deeply moving experience. The veil is lifting. The moment has come for the unfolding of the end-time visions. As I contemplated this, I fell on my knees and worshipped God. God is holy. His name is Yea and Amen; that which He says and prophesies always comes to pass.

Today we can see the truth of His words. We have entered an age of fear and dread. Iniquity is sweeping through every country. Terrorism, rumours of war, calamities, famine and death rule the earth, because it is polluted by sin, lawlessness and rebellion. Blasphemies are pervading heathen and anti-Christian nations; they are also spreading throughout the so-called Christian nations. Even in groups of committed Christians, blasphemous productions are permitted.[1] "Down with God!" is the shout being raised in Christian nations. Sin is mounting up everywhere in the world and crying out to heaven. Even now the Harlot of Babylon, the apostate Church, is raising her head. She is in alliance with the beast, which is covered with blasphemies. The nations of the earth are drinking from her cup and becoming intoxicated by her wine of immorality, as John saw in his vision (Revelation 17:3 ff.).[2]

The sins of the nations are crying out to heaven, and now the answer must come. The judgment of God is inevitable. The sword issuing from Jesus' mouth will descend (Revelation 1:16). The age of God's wrath has commenced; we are living in the pre-antichristian era. The time is near when the countenance of the Saviour, the meek and patient Lamb, will become that of the wrathful Lamb. At the frightening sight of His countenance men will cry out to the mountains and rocks, "Fall on us and hide us from the face of him who is seated on the throne, and from the wrath of the Lamb" (Revelation 6:16).

Jesus was gracious to the Apostle John, because he fell on the ground before Him in humility and holy fear, and He will also be gracious to us if we truly humble ourselves. Whoever lies before God as a penitent sinner, willing to forgive others just as he was forgiven by Jesus, will be spared the sword of judgment. True, many faithful believers will meet death, but not by the sword of divine wrath and judgment. They will be killed by the sword of God-haters and die as martyrs. Indeed, when sin and lawlessness gain the upper hand, the blood of the martyrs will flow, because Satan hates Jesus and His disciples. This era has already commenced. Even now hatred and persecution of Christians is spreading through many parts of the world – and no country will be exempt. Therefore, I felt constrained to pray:

> Prepare me, Lord Jesus. Help me to so live my life today that I can suffer for You tomorrow.

When the Apocalypse was made known to John almost 2,000 years ago, God in His great love was already thinking of us, who would be living in this age and who would have to undergo the sufferings of the pre-antichristian times. Accordingly He provided the help we need in the Apocalypse, which is *the* book for us today.

Now when the Apocalypse is beginning to be fulfilled in our day, God's own are being challenged, "Prepare yourselves. Time is short. The judgment of God is threatening to descend." There in the grotto on the island of Patmos my heart was so gripped by the urgency of the hour that I began to write. The Lord opened my eyes to see the significance of the final conflict between light and darkness, the battle between the two kingdoms and the two armies in the end times. He showed me the reality of the wrath of God and His judgments – but also the different groups of overcomers in the heavenly glory, as they are described in Revelation. For the Apocalypse does not merely present the coming diabolical horrors, the devastating power of Satan and his onslaughts against the disciples of Jesus. It is the only book in the Bible that tells us about the City of God and its ineffable beauty, the pilgrim's shining goal, which gives him the strength to endure in the darkest of vales. It is the book that unmasks the "beast" and makes Jesus, the Lamb of God, shine forth all the more radiantly in enthralling beauty, victorious might and majesty at the throne of glory, as the Sun of righteousness, the Light illumining the City of God. My heart was overwhelmed. Who can compare with the Lamb of God! The Lamb will put an end to all the raging and deceptions of the beast as well as to his power on earth. By His patient, enduring love and sacrificial death the Lamb will establish His victory in triumph. He will bring to consummation all God's plans for the earth and mankind.

The Apocalypse, which Jesus received from the Father and which John passed on to the world, is meant above all for us, the generation of the end times. Therefore, "blessed is he that readeth, and they that hear the words of this prophecy, and keep those things which are written therein: for the time is at hand" (Revelation 1:3 AV).

The following pages, written on the island of Patmos, are not intended to be a textbook on Revelation; nor are they an attempt to interpret everything in it. Rather this book is meant to shed light upon that which is of importance for us in the times we are living in. The great prophecy that John received for the end times is now beginning to be fulfilled in our generation. Therefore, this book is intended to offer comfort and strength in this satanic age of horrors and afflictions. As I read the Book of Revelation, one thought illumined my heart like a bright star:

> His purposes are truly wonderful, and He leads all things to a marvellous end – to victory and consummation. He will lead us too through suffering into glory beyond compare.

The End Times — The Highest Heavens and the Deepest Depths Are Opened

The end times — a time when all former standards have ceased to exist. There are only two extremes to choose from with nothing in between. As Revelation shows us, only two alternatives exist: the supreme glory of heaven at the throne, the City of God, and the uttermost depths of hell, the lake of fire.

The end times — a time of division. Some will ascend and reach the highest heaven, whereas the others will fall down into the deepest abyss of hell. Everything will come to full maturity during the deceptions of the end times and later during the judgments of wrath. Figuratively speaking, the hearts of men can be compared to fruit. If a small worm eats its way into a piece of fruit, it begins to rot. In former times this was scarcely noticeable on the outside. But in the end times the deceptions and severe trials make the secret things of the heart, be they good or bad, ripen quickly and become visible to the eye. If a person does not have the small worm in his heart cut out at the beginning, he will find that his fruit has turned rotten overnight. Such a person did not accept the chastenings of God. He was not determined to take the commandments of God as absolutely binding and to fight a battle of prayer and faith against sin to the point of shedding blood. Now in the end times our innermost hearts are laid bare — that is, our relationship to Jesus and thus our attitude to our sin. Sin has become visible. This explains why all of a sudden we see countless numbers of people whose faces bear the mark of sin and whose personalities are ruined.

But just as a large percentage of mankind today is ripening into bad fruit and becoming enslaved to Satan and a prey of hell, since they give free rein to sin, there is a small group of people that is ripening into good fruit. They will attain the highest degree of glory in heaven. These are people who would not tolerate the small worm in their hearts; ever anew they let their sins be washed away by the blood of the Lamb. And as a result they have become beautiful fruit, sweet and succulent, their colouring enhanced by rain and sunshine.

Today it is either all or nothing. "Total" is the word. These believers are experiencing total redemption and transformation into the image of Jesus (though they remain sinful beings to the end of their lives). They are being purified by all the suffering they have to undergo in the end times. And the many trials and temptations in the satanic age of deception that they must withstand only serve to make them overcomers, because they must persevere and keep faith in the battle against sin and Satan.

But even among believers there are many who let themselves be increasingly drawn into Satan's snares until he finally takes complete control of them. Because they live a life detached from the commandments of God, they commit all manner of sins. Thus these people, who once acknowledged Jesus as their Lord and Saviour, increasingly bear the characteristics of Satan.

Let us heed the mighty voice of the angel, who in the end times flies through the heavens, calling men to fear God, that is, to turn from their wicked ways (Revelation 14:6 f.). His summons is meant for us. Today everything is at stake. Either we attain the supreme joy of heaven or else we fall into the deepest abyss of hell. Therefore, let us turn our eyes heavenward. Let us read and hear about those who attained heaven and commit ourselves fully to follow the same pathway.

Indeed, it is as if the overcomers are beckoning us from above, saying, "We are waiting for you. The last hour has come. There is little time left for you to prepare yourselves." This calls for our utmost resolution. Jesus must be our sole desire and we must be determined to follow His commandments unconditionally in every area of our lives. This requires an all-out effort on our part. We must battle even to the point of bloodshed, firmly believing in Jesus' victory, calling upon His name and claiming His blood. For if the Apostle Paul, who was a devoted follower of Jesus and a chosen one of God, had to strive to attain the heavenly prize (Philippians 3:12), how can we attain this goal unless we too have given our total effort?

Amid the tribulations of the end times Jesus reveals the glory of heaven to us in the Apocalypse, so that we shall strive for this goal. He shows us that heaven awaits those who have endured severe hardships and the onslaughts of Satan. After the time of affliction, the heavens will open to receive them for all eternity. In an age bearing satanic characteristics Jesus grants His own a glimpse of heaven and its splendour, so that they will be drawn by its radiance. With such a glorious goal before us, all suffering becomes insignificant and worth enduring. Heaven is beckoning. Above there is everlasting joy and glory with Jesus. This knowledge is to give us the strength to bear pain and anguish, so that we who have to live through the end times shall be able to endure, yes, be victorious in all suffering.

The apocalyptic age, like the Apocalypse itself, does not only speak of terrors, judgment and the beast of the abyss. In the same degree that hell is revealing itself today and becoming a reality for man, heaven also is to become a reality for us – indeed, more of a reality than ever. Although the earth has never witnessed such a manifestation of hell before, now in the end times we are to experience an awe-inspiring manifestation of heaven, which is greater still.

"The age of St. Stephen" has dawned. In other words, we have not only entered the age of horrors, darkness, persecution, torture and martyrdom, but like Stephen, whose face was radiant because he saw the open heavens when he was being stoned to death, we too are to see the open heavens. In the apocalyptic age, God's children turn their eyes towards heaven; then heaven opens and shines upon them. When they experience hatred, wickedness, malevolence and torture, they are immersed in heaven's glory, in the love of Jesus and His divine radiance. Heaven will not remain inactive when the forces of hell are unleashed and people have to taste hell on earth. Heaven will prove that it is stronger, just as Jesus is stronger than Satan, who is but a created being, a fallen angel. Heaven will demonstrate that it has a wealth of joy, peace and comfort to give to those who believe in Jesus and His victory. Whoever believes that the glory of heaven can shine into this age of darkness will experience that all earthly sorrows are drowned by the joy of heaven.

Heaven, like hell, as the Apocalypse shows us, opens up in the end times. Hell devours everyone who previously allowed it to enter his life. Conversely, heaven opens up and imparts its glory to all those who open their hearts to heaven, making the City of God their only goal, determined to reach it at all costs. Their thoughts dwell upon heaven and upon those who have already attained the goal of glory, who were gathered as good, ripe fruit by the angels and brought into the heavenly garner at the end of their earthly lives. Their aim is to be like these overcomers at the throne, and they want to follow the same pathway, knowing that it will lead them to the supreme goal.

The Different Groups of Overcomers
at the Throne of the Lamb

In Revelation Jesus shows us the different groups of
overcomers in the heavenly glory. It is as if they, the
church triumphant, are greeting us, the church militant;
for have they not come out of great suffering such as we
now have to endure? Their radiance is to shine into our
darkness and enthral our hearts. When reading the Book
of Revelation, we can sense how all the groups standing
round the throne of God are immersed in His divine
splendour and filled with supreme joy. They are now
with the Lord in ineffable glory – for ever and ever.
All have one thing in common – they are overcomers.
However, each specific group has a different rôle and
experiences the heavenly glory in a different way.

The Singers on the Sea of Glass

And I saw as it were a sea of glass mingled with fire:
and them that had gotten the victory over the beast, and
over his image, and over his mark, and over the number
of his name, stand on the sea of glass, having the harps
of God. And they sing the song of Moses the servant of
God, and the song of the Lamb, saying, Great and
marvellous are thy works, Lord God Almighty; just and
true are thy ways, thou King of saints. Who shall not
fear thee, O Lord, and glorify thy name? for thou only
art holy: for all nations shall come and worship before
thee; for thy judgments are made manifest.
                                        Revelation 15:2-4 AV

What a glorious throng! The singers on the sea of glass
show us how the glory of heaven, which they now
reflect, was able to drive away the gruesomeness of the

18

dark world from which they came. The light of God and the divine world shone so brightly into their lives that its radiance rendered the darkness of the antichristian era ineffective.

The singers on the sea of glass are martyrs. In Revelation 15:2 it is written that they won the victory over the beast and his image and the number denoting his name. They took up the battle against Satan; otherwise it could not be said that they were victorious over the beast. How did they gain the victory? By refusing to comply with the demands of rulers who were hostile towards Jesus. They did not worship the Antichrist and his image; nor did they allow themselves to be marked with his number, which everyone who wished to buy or sell had to bear on his forehead or hand. As a result they were doomed to die. Because everyone who refused to worship the beast was put to death (Revelation 13:15), they had entered a battle that would cost them their lives. Indeed, "they loved not their lives even unto death" (Revelation 12:11), rather they loved Jesus. Their love for Jesus was so strong that they were even willing to die for Him, and therefore Satan could not claim them as his prey. Indeed, by this love they were able to overcome Satan and be victorious. In spite of all the dangers they were uncompromising in their witness. Out of love for Jesus, they testified that He is the King of kings and Son of God, their Lord and Saviour. The blood of the Lamb gave them the strength to resist Satan, to profess their faith and remain steadfast, even when it meant suffering torment and bitter death. What a triumph! This is how they won the victory – a victory that gained them ineffable glory for all eternity.

In the City of God they now taste this glory, which is promised to the overcomers. But this is not all! They are standing on the sea of glass. What this really means we can see from Revelation 4:6. "Before the throne there is as it were a sea of glass, like crystal." Thus the singers on the sea of glass have their place directly before the divine throne, where the Holy Trinity is seated in great glory and majesty. What a privilege it is to be so close to God the Father! They are permitted to see Him enthroned on high – the holy, almighty and immortal God, who holds the government of the whole world in His hands, and yet who as the God of love became their Father through our Lord Jesus Christ. They are also permitted to behold Jesus enthroned as the King of kings arrayed in majesty, glory and magnificent beauty.

The sea of glass mirrors the divine beauty and glory of God. It is pervaded with light, bright and shining like crystal, as pure and transparent as the thoughts and plans of God, which are of indescribable wisdom, clarity and truth. When the Bible says that the sea of glass is mingled with fire, it can be taken as an illustration of God's leadings in the lives of the overcomers. They had to pass through the fire of trials and temptations, but these were woven into the marvellous, crystal-like plans of God. And now they stand on a sea of light and glory.

There the singers are playing the most glorious music on their harps as they raise their voices in song before the throne. And the sound of this heavenly music is so enthralling that in the other spheres of heaven everyone who hears the vibrant chords of the harps and the jubilant voices is overwhelmed with delight. In their anthems the singers worship God and His perfect ways.

How did this throng overcome in their great affliction, in their battle with Satan? By their total dedication to the Lord, which they expressed in two specific songs of praise and adoration. But they did not learn these two songs in heaven; they had sung them on earth. For in heaven we can sing only that which we have already practised on earth in the midst of suffering. Having come out of great affliction, they praise God in their first song, the Song of Moses, declaring how just and perfect His ways are. In doing so, they follow the example of Moses. Although he had to tread such hard and bitter ways through the wilderness, ways fraught with inner conflict and suffering, he worshipped God with the words, "Your work is perfect; for all Your ways are justice. Ascribe greatness to our God!" (cf. Deuteronomy 32:3 f.). It is as if these overcomers are singing this song to us, their brothers here on earth. For we are a generation that is being led along especially hard paths; many are suffering martyrdom or approaching it.

With their song they seek to help us, who are still on earth, to overcome in all the suffering of the end times that we have to undergo. For if we begin to praise and worship God for His love at such times when we are sorely tempted to doubt His love, we shall drive away Satan, who continually seeks to evoke from our hearts the question, "Why do we have to suffer so much?" The power of Satan is broken when a person clings to the love of God in the hour of temptation and dire distress and honours God by singing in praise, "My Father, I trust You, even if I can no longer understand You."

This is what the singers on the sea of glass had done. Because their hearts were filled with loving trust as well as dedication to suffering, they won the victory over Satan. And therefore they sing, "Great and wonderful are thy deeds, O Lord God the Almighty! Just and true are thy ways, O King of the ages! Who shall not fear and glorify thy name, O Lord?" (Revelation 15:3 f.). This they declared, although they could have lost their confidence in God, for not only had they seen how Satan and evil were given complete victory over the believers throughout the world, but they had also suffered much personally. They were hated, wronged, persecuted and killed, because they did not go along with the general trend to discard the commandments. In their holy reverence and fear of God they did not abandon His ordinances nor cease to testify to Him even when it cost them their lives. Affliction was their daily fare. Nevertheless they did not ask, "Why?" Rather they said ever anew, "Just and true are thy ways." They were utterly convinced that even if, as mere created beings, we cannot know what plans of God are behind everything that happens, we can trust that they are good.

"Just and true are thy ways!" This was their testimony before the visible and invisible world. With these words they worshipped Jesus and God the Father as the One who alone is true and holy. They recognized Satan as a deceiver and liar and saw through his devious schemes when, with his instruments, he posed as an angel of light, pretending to bring peace and salvation, righteousness and freedom. Filled with awe by the fact that God alone is true and holy, they praise Him for His holiness even if He did not exert His power on their behalf. They worship Him as the almighty God, compared to whom Satan with his great display of power is a mere nothing despite the fact that he appeared to be winning the victory and even put Jesus' disciples to death. In triumph they declare, "All nations shall come and worship thee!" (Revelation 15:4).

The overcomers on the sea of glass also sing another song, the Song of the Lamb. This too they had sung on earth, because they were wholly dedicated to Jesus and followed Him, the Lamb. The song that the Lamb of God raised on His earthly pathway had but one theme, "Give Me the cross to bear, for I will bear it gladly; not My will, but Thine, be done!" Fully committed to the will of the Father and dedicated to suffering, Jesus submitted to the blows and wounds of wicked men — men to whom He had given His love and for whom

He laid down His life. Indeed, Jesus permitted Himself to be tortured and led to the slaughter as the Lamb that did not open His mouth before the shearers. Likewise the sole response of the singers on the sea of glass to all the suffering that God laid upon them was, "All Your leadings are just and right; I will gladly bear the suffering." The love of the Lamb radiated from them as they faced their tormentors, and by this love they were even able to win some of them for the Lord. In suffering they became so like Jesus that they can now be with Him in glory for ever.

This is why they now stand as victors on the sea of glass. We can imagine how they praise God ever anew, their hearts overflowing with thanksgiving, "By leading us along hard and incomprehensible paths of suffering, You brought us here, to this glory at Your throne, O Father of love." They, who had inflicted wounds upon Jesus with their sins and then let wounds be inflicted upon themselves for His name's sake, now sing the Song of the Lamb for all eternity. In the choir of worshippers at the throne they praise Him – filled with the joyous assurance that soon, very soon all mankind and all created beings in heaven and on earth and under the earth will join in the Song of the Lamb. The victorious throng on the sea of glass rejoices in fervent gratitude, "The blood of the Lamb has gotten us the victory!" For they have triumphed over the beast.

These songs of adoration are so glorious that they are able to dispel the temptations of those who have to live on earth during the pre-antichristian and antichristian era with all its horrors and darkness. When the dragon is victorious everywhere, when there seems to be no limit to his power, and when the whole world and all mankind are under his dominion, plunged into unspeakable misery and distress, let us heed the summons from above, "Worship God and sing the two songs ever anew. For

23

in the Song of Moses and the Song of the Lamb you will receive the strength you need to overcome."

Indeed, by their example the singers on the sea of glass challenge us:

> In all the small trials and vexations of everyday life sing the song of total submission to God's ways and deeds, even when they go against your will. Then in the darkest night of suffering in the satanic era, you will be able to sing the Song of Moses and the Lamb, the song of complete dedication to the ways and will of God. And you will have the strength to commit yourselves to the severe suffering in the time of martyrdom and thus gain the victory over Satan instead of falling into his clutches. Then you will be able to overcome and one day stand on the sea of glass in inconceivable glory.

Their testimony contains another challenge for us:

> Take care never to deny the name of Jesus. Rather out of love for Him confess His name and take a stand for Him whenever He is attacked and blasphemed today. Practise now. Then you will be able to testify to the name of Jesus when it means anguish and torture – yes, even death. Now, while it is still possible, it is vital to pass on the testimony of His name by the spoken and written word, letting no opportunity slip by, even if it may have serious consequences for you.
>
> Do not love your life, but lay it down every day anew – out of love for Jesus. Die to your ego with all its demands and desires. Die to self and overcome all fear of the cross by dedicating yourselves to suffering and all that is hard for you to bear in

everyday life. Then you will also be able to lay down your life for Jesus in martyrdom.

Today when persecution is imminent, the martyrs, the singers on the sea of glass, are a powerful challenge to us, for many of us are to belong to their number in heaven. No time is to be lost. Now we must practise treading the same pathway they took. And just as they won the victory over the beast, so must we, who are living at the beginning of the end times, gain the victory over his predecessors, the forerunners of the Antichrist. Everything depends upon this, for the Lord sent His angel to proclaim:

> "If any one worships the beast and its image, and receives a mark on his forehead or on his hand, he also shall drink the wine of God's wrath, poured unmixed into the cup of his anger, and he shall be tormented with fire and brimstone in the presence of the holy angels and in the presence of the Lamb. And the smoke of their torment goes up for ever and ever; and they have no rest, day or night, these worshippers of the beast and its image, and whoever receives the mark of its name."
>
> Revelation 14:9-11

What a terrible judgment of wrath will descend upon those who sought to preserve their lives! They denied the name of Jesus by worshipping the beast and letting his mark be placed upon their forehead or hand so as to escape torture and a bitter death.

The die is being cast now as to whether we shall be strong and victorious in the hour of extreme temptation when our decision will determine our eternal destiny. If we practise surrendering our wills now, dying to self and testifying courageously day by day, we shall be strong and able to stand firm in the time of suffering that lies before us. Then we shall be overcomers in the time of persecution and martyrdom and attain the crown of life (Revelation 2:10). The singers on the sea of glass are waiting for their number to be completed. And how Jesus must be yearning for this moment too, for then He can come again in glory and Satan can be destroyed! Who will be privileged to join the overcomers on the sea of glass and sing their song with them?

Prayer of Dedication to the Will of God
Eternal, great, most high and mighty God,

I humbly lie before You — wholly submitted to Your majesty, to Your will. Your will is holy to me and worthy to be praised, for it is pure love. I surrender my will to You in complete trust. Whatever You send into my life I will accept, humbling myself beneath Your hand. I will worship You for it, for Your will is always good and Your eternal wisdom has planned the best for me.

Perfect are Your ways; just and righteous are Your judgments, O eternal God! You lead Your saints wonderfully to the goal of everlasting glory, and You have ordained my paths according to Your eternal plan of love. In heaven above I shall praise and worship the wisdom of Your thoughts, the glory of Your deeds and the fulfilment of Your purposes for ever and ever. Amen

Prayer of Dedication to Suffering
My Lord Jesus,

You make me strong and steadfast, courageous of heart, aflame with love and burning with dedication to You. You make me hard as granite with the determination: I desire Jesus and nothing but Jesus!

I am ready to suffer for You. I do not seek relief, nor do I wish to have the comfort of seeing and feeling

All I desire is to embrace You in faith, to love You and suffer for You, Jesus, in the midst of darkness and temptation.   Amen

M. Martyria Madauss

Prayer for a Courageous Witness
Lord Jesus,

Grant me that which I lack — fearlessness and the courage to witness out of love for You. You have promised to answer our prayers. This I believe and I know that by Your Holy Spirit You will empower me and give me the courage to witness.

My Lord Jesus, I will fix my eyes upon the goal above. Soon suffering will be over and transformed into glory, and I shall be at Your side for ever.   Amen

The Multitude Clothed in White Robes

After this I looked, and behold, a great multitude which no man could number, from every nation, from all tribes and peoples and tongues, standing before the throne and before the Lamb, clothed in white robes, with palm branches in their hands, and crying out with a loud voice, "Salvation belongs to our God who sits upon the throne, and to the Lamb!" And all the angels stood round the throne and round the elders and the four living creatures, and they fell on their faces before the throne and worshipped God, saying, "Amen! Blessing and glory and wisdom and thanksgiving and honour and power and might be to our God for ever and ever! Amen."

Then one of the elders addressed me, saying, "Who are these, clothed in white robes, and whence have they come?" I said to him, "Sir, you know." And he said to me, "These are they who have come out of the great tribulation; they have washed their robes and made them white in the blood of the Lamb. Therefore are they before the throne of God, and serve him day and night within his temple; and he who sits upon the throne will shelter them with his presence. They shall hunger no more, neither thirst any more; the sun shall not strike them, nor any scorching heat. For the Lamb in the midst of the throne will be their shepherd, and he will guide them to springs of living water; and God will wipe away every tear from their eyes."   Revelation 7:9-17

Heaven opens up further; that which is hidden is unveiled and we can see another group of overcomers. It seems as though they too are beckoning and calling to us, "Choose our path, and you will be with the Lamb above in glory."

A great multitude gathered from every nation stands before the throne and the Lamb, most of them coming probably from the pre-antichristian and antichristian era. They had suffered the fears and terrors of their age. They had undergone deep anguish in a world deluged with sin, deceptions, lawlessness and diabolical horrors; and in addition they had endured severe persecution. Now they are attired in white and hold palm branches in their hands. With a loud voice they cry, "Salvation belongs to our God who sits upon the throne, and to the Lamb!"

Jesus had promised these overcomers in dazzling white robes that they would walk with Him above (Revelation 3:4). What a magnificent sight! They walk on golden streets of brilliant splendour at Jesus' side, clad in robes of shining white linen. Of God Himself it is written in Daniel 7, "His raiment was white as snow" (verse 9). During the Transfiguration the disciples saw Jesus in shining white raiment. And now those who have overcome are endowed with the same nobility as the Lamb — they have become like unto Him. In eternity our inner life becomes visible. The overcomers wear a robe that shows how they had lived their lives. All that

28

they had done in this life, all their struggles, their contrition and their victories are displayed in the sight of the whole world for eternity. Never will they have to remove this white robe; never will it become stained or soiled, for it is made out of an imperishable material of eternal beauty.

How was it that they came to receive this glorious garment? It was awarded to them by Jesus, who had procured it for them by His suffering and by His outpoured blood. And yet they had to do their part, as it is written, "They have washed their robes and made them white in the blood of the Lamb" (Revelation 7:14). Their constant desire was to make their soiled clothes white and this determined everything they did on earth. Ever anew they washed their clothes in the blood of the Lamb.

In other words, these overcomers were taken up with one thought – to attain the white robe, no matter what the cost and to stand one day before the throne of the Lamb clad in white. Therefore, they gave their utmost, not heeding the suffering and battles that ensued. Although no details are given, we know that this group comes out of great affliction. Yet is it not amazing that despite the trials they had to endure, it was something else that captivated their attention? To attain the white robe was of greater urgency and importance to them than all the suffering.

When we consider how easily we Christians become preoccupied with suffering and so burdened down by it that we have no room in our hearts for anything else, we can understand what is so special about this group. When we are in suffering, we usually pay little attention to the stains of sin in our nature. We do not weep over them, but over our suffering. Yet actually it stands to reason that we should pay much greater attention to our sinful stains. The suffering of this life is transient. But sin – if it is not washed away by the blood of the Lamb – will bring us suffering for all eternity.

In connection with these white robes Jesus says in Revelation 3:3 to the leader of the church at Sardis, "If you will not awake, I will come like a thief, and you will not know at what hour I will come upon you." In what respect had the leader of the church not been awake? The answer is found in the following words, "You have still a few names in Sardis, people who have not soiled their garments; and they shall walk with me in white, for they are worthy" (verse 4). That is to say, he had not watched over the members of his congregation; he had not noticed that many of them had soiled the white garment that they had received through the forgiveness of their sins in the blood of the Lamb at their conversion and rebirth. And the stains remained, because they did not wash them in the blood of the Lamb. If they had come to Jesus with their sins and washed their robes in the blood of the Lamb, as the overcomers in Revelation 7 had done, their robes would have become white again. However, there were only a few at Sardis whose robes were not stained, and therefore Jesus gives the leader the challenge, "He that overcometh, the same shall be clothed in white raiment" (Revelation 3:5 av).

The group of overcomers in Revelation 7 is an illustration of this Bible verse. They were intent on receiving the white garment and were careful not to let any stain of sin remain in their lives. Thus they washed their robes in the blood of the Lamb. But when do we wash a garment? When we see stains on it. Thus if we wish to walk in white at Jesus' side, we must first receive light so as to really see our stains of sin. This is no matter of course, for by nature we are very blind to our sins. He who does not see his sins does not ask Jesus to wash them away with His blood, and thus they remain for ever.

We shall not be cleansed automatically. The redemptive blood of Jesus is of no avail for us if we do not claim His redemption and His blood, if we think that we do not need His holy blood and that it is not necessary to wash our robes because we can find no spot on them.

Therefore let our prayer be:

> Give me Your light.
> Without Your help I'm sightless.
> Dear Lord, I'm blind –
> My natural eyes are useless.
> O let me see.

> Give me Your light.
> Lord, grant me this concession.
> Heal all my blindness;
> Show me my transgression.
> O give me light.

> Give me Your light.
> And do not let it spare me.
> Show me my sin
> And true repentance grant me.
> Then I'll be free.*

The overcomers in white robes had received light about themselves. They were alert and not asleep. Consequently they saw the stains on their garments, which can be seen only in daylight. Unlike many other believers, they could not bear to wear stained garments. They knew that they could not appear before the holy God nor dwell in His city in soiled garments, for there, only light and purity are admitted. It is written of the

* *In the Name of Jesus* (prayers and songs for the battle of faith), no. 1.

City of God, "Nothing unclean shall enter it" (Revelation 21:27). This is why they were intent on attaining the white robe, which is granted to those who have emerged victorious from the battle against sin. As they struggled on in the midst of suffering, their primary concern was not that they would be delivered from the suffering, but rather that the stains of sin would be removed from their garments. Had not Jesus said unequivocally, ". . . evil thoughts, murder, adultery, fornication, theft, false witness, slander. These are what defile a man" (Matthew 15:19 f.)? Accordingly, they hated everything that defiles the nature of man.

As we have seen, the distinctive feature of this group is that they did not let themselves be dominated by suffering, even though it was bitterly hard for them to live on earth in the end times – a feeling we can understand now that the earth is becoming more and more like hell and the persecution of God's own is increasing. But all the suffering that normally would cause hearts to despair was unable to oppress them. They were not crushed by the afflictions of the end times. True, they suffered immeasurably, because sin had established its terrible rule over mankind and was raising its head against God and His commandments. However, this suffering did not cast them into a state of depression and despondency; rather it spurred them on to take measures. Their motto was, "Sin, which has such dreadful consequences and causes God immeasurable grief, cannot remain in our lives. It must be overcome."

They fought their battle with great ardour, because they longed for Jesus to receive them as overcomers and grant them the white robe and the palm branch, the symbol of victory. What did their battle entail? They hated sin and refused to tolerate it. They could not bear the slightest stain on their robes – an unkind word, an unfriendly glance, impure thoughts, bitterness, covetousness, untruthfulness or any other sin that defiles us. For this reason they did not cover up anything, nor did they deny their faults to themselves and others. Rather each time they discovered a stain, they brought it into the light and confessed it before God and man. And when others brought stains to their attention, they accepted the admonishment gratefully. Then they hastened to Jesus with their sins and washed their robes in His blood. The blood of the Lamb had become very precious to them. They would sing in praise, "The blood of the Lamb cleanses us from every sin." But they did not merely know of the power in Jesus' blood; they claimed it in their battles and immersed their faults and sinful nature in His blood. And since they washed their dirty robes white in the blood of the Lamb, no one can condemn them.[3, 4]

Because they hastened to Jesus with every stain that each new day left on their robes, they were close to the Lamb of God in this life and therefore they are close to Him above. Indeed, they are a part of Him, for even in this life the Lamb of God, who shed His innocent blood for us, was their Love. To Him they rendered all their thanksgiving and adoration. And their songs of praise continue in heaven, for they have experienced that Jesus' promise has come true and that as overcomers they have actually received the white robes. Now for all eternity they are clad in white.

Tribulation helped them to gain the victory. For in suffering we cannot be deceived about ourselves; suffering reveals our true nature. It lays bare all rebelliousness, impatience, lack of dedication to the will of God, unwillingness to suffer, irritation and despondency. A Christian of our times who had been sentenced to a concentration camp testified that not only were they physically unclothed, but soul and spirit were also laid bare. Either their sinful attributes came to the light or their

3

power to overcome. It became apparent who was a hypocrite and who was a true believer. No one could hide his true nature any longer. All of a sudden the difference between the believers was like day and night. For now that which actually filled their hearts became evident. They had all experienced conversion at one time. But some of them had kept their stains and in this severe suffering their unredeemed nature gained the upper hand. The others had claimed Jesus' redemptive power. He alone filled their hearts. His divine life now demonstrated its might in them and became victorious. Suffering lost its power. Now the words of Scripture came true, "Blessed are those who mourn, for they shall be comforted" (Matthew 5:4).

Thus it was the affliction and manifold suffering they had to undergo that helped the souls in Revelation 7 to become overcomers. It helped them ever anew to see the stains on their robes and to wash them in the blood of the Lamb. Let us, therefore, heed their challenge:

Do not let suffering weigh you down. When the waves of affliction surge over you, do not let them drown you. It is Satan's objective to make suffering defeat you. Therefore, be alert. Resist him in combat. Do not let the suffering engross you. Rather, let the stains in your garment be your real sorrow. Keep fighting against sin and wash your robes in the blood of the Lamb ever anew. Let this be your main concern. The time of affliction will be over one day and with it the things that are often hard on earth: making a painful admission of guilt or a confession of sin, asking forgiveness and setting things right. However, the privilege of walking in white with Jesus on the golden streets of His city in His glory will be for all eternity.

Just as the Song of the Lamb and of His committal to suffering is the special characteristic of the singers on the sea of glass, the special feature of the group of overcomers clad in white is that they praise the blood of the Lamb. In each case it is a close relationship to the Lamb of God that characterizes these groups of overcomers. And for this reason they are privileged to be with the Lamb in His glory for all eternity. They loved the Lamb of God with all their heart. They lived by His strength. He was their help and protection in the time of affliction. It was His song that they sang, and by His blood they were victorious.

> Your blood has pow'r to rescue us
> From Satan's might and craftiness.
> O Lamb of God, Your blood I praise;
> It works such miracles of grace.
>
> Your blood, O Lord, was shed for me;
> Accept my thanks eternally.
> I praise Your blood, O Lamb of God,
> By which such miracles are wrought.
>
> Your blood will make me pure within
> And cleanse my blood of every sin.
> O Lamb of God, Your blood I praise;
> It works such miracles of grace.
>
> What harm can Satan do to me?
> Christ Jesus won the victory!
> He shed His blood to save my soul,
> To ransom me and make me whole.*

---

* More songs for the battle of faith can be found in *7 X around the Walls of Jericho*.

The 144,000 on Mount Zion

Then I looked, and lo, on Mount Zion stood the Lamb, and with him a hundred and forty-four thousand who had his name and his Father's name written on their foreheads. And I heard a voice from heaven like the sound of many waters and like the sound of loud thunder; the voice I heard was like the sound of harpers playing on their harps, and they sang a new song before the throne and before the four living creatures and before the elders. No one could learn that song except the hundred and forty-four thousand who had been redeemed from the earth. It is these who have not defiled themselves with women, for they are chaste; it is these who follow the Lamb wherever he goes; these have been redeemed from mankind as first fruits for God and the Lamb, and in their mouth no lie was found, for they are spotless.   Revelation 14:1-5

Once again heaven opens and another group is revealed to John. They are standing round the Lamb, gathered on Mount Zion, by which the City of God is probably meant. They are not an innumerable multitude from all nations and races, but a numbered group, the 144,000. This throng consists solely of the first-born, who had been redeemed from mankind as firstfruits for God and the Lamb. The firstfruits from the land were regarded by the children of Israel as an especially precious offering for the Lord – but even more so their first-born sons, who had to be redeemed from the Temple, since they belonged to God. He had chosen them. One could say that the words "set apart" were invisibly written upon them. They were consecrated to God, set apart for Him, so as to live for Him alone. Thus all those who belong to the firstfruits standing by the Lamb on Mount Zion are in a special sense chosen ones of God. They were wholly consecrated to Him. They were chosen out of all other believers just like the tribe of Levi, which was chosen out of all the other tribes of Israel to be a tribe of priests, to minister to the Lord alone, to serve Him in the sanctuary and have no other inheritance among their brothers.

Everything that is said of this group on Mount Zion shows us the characteristics distinguishing them as first-fruits. Like the singers on the sea of glass the 144,000 will have sung the Song of the Lamb, and they will have washed themselves in the blood of the Lamb as the great multitude before the throne did. Yet something else is related about them. They have the name of the Lamb and His Father written on their foreheads like a seal signifying that they are consecrated to the Lamb, consecrated to the Bridegroom, Jesus Christ. The seal also signifies that their whole nature and being bears the characteristics of the Lamb of God. They are, as the Apostle Paul once wrote, "of his flesh, and of his bones" (Ephesians 5:30 AV) – completely one with Jesus and His nature.

This election and sealing took place before the anti-christian era began. In Revelation 7:1-8 we read that 144,000 from the tribes of Israel were sealed. The first-fruits, therefore, are comprised of bridal souls from among the Jews, and in addition, bridal souls gathered from the Gentile believers, who according to Romans 11 have been grafted into the stock of Israel. Together they make up the "bride of the Lamb". The New Jerusalem, which is the bride (Revelation 21), is inhabited by members of the people of Israel, for the foundations of the walls are the Apostles (Revelation 21:14), who will rule the tribes of Israel (Matthew 19:28). But the City of God is also inhabited by believers from the nations from all centuries, for in the letters to the seven churches Jesus says to Gentile believers, "He who conquers, I will grant him to sit with me on my throne and I will write on him the name of the New Jerusalem" (cf. Revelation 3:12, 21).

The 144,000 are a throng of chosen souls. They were chosen by God and they responded by making God their sole choice. "God alone" was their motto. Their whole heart was aflame with love for Jesus, their Bridegroom. Their lives were not torn by conflicting interests nor was their love divided between Jesus and their dear ones. They did not seek Jesus *and* the fulfilment of their earthly desires, Jesus *and* prestige, popularity, etc. They had but one desire and that was to love Jesus and to glorify Him, to suffer for Him and give Him all they possessed – above all, themselves. This is why it is written, "It is these who have not defiled themselves with women, for they are virgins." And Paul once mentioned that he was zealous for the members of his church at Corinth, because he had betrothed her to Christ to present her as a pure bride to her one husband (2 Corinthians 11:2).

Like pure virgins who love their bridegroom alone, the 144,000 love Jesus above all else and are solely enthralled by Him. These are souls who have kept themselves undefiled by the world and who permitted no one and nothing to enter their hearts that could bind or captivate them in any way. They had but one love, and that was Jesus, their Bridegroom. For this reason they could not do otherwise than follow the Lamb wherever He went. They had committed themselves to Jesus like a wife to her husband. Inseparably united with Him, they followed His pathway. And thus as the bride of the Lamb they went the way of the Lamb.

The pathway the Lamb of God followed on earth was marked by the cross – that is, by lowliness, poverty, obedience and self-denial. The typical characteristic of the firstfruits was that they freely chose the very thing that others, including believers, often seek to evade – the way of the cross. That which is bitter for other believers became sweet for them – pathways of self-denial, lowliness, poverty and deprivation. They were willing to do without honour and forgo that which would have brought fulfilment to their lives on a human level. However, it was not asceticism, but love for the Lamb of God that made them choose His pathway. Yes, of their own free will they chose His pathway – this was the special thing about them. In everyday life they shared this path with their Bridegroom, constrained by love. They had consecrated themselves to Jesus and committed themselves to share His path and to follow Him wherever He would lead them.[5]

Scripture also tells us that no lie or falsehood was found upon their lips. That is to say, they had no ulterior motive whatsoever; they were completely truthful. Their hearts were wholly transparent and overflowing with love for Jesus. They were single-hearted in their desire to please and glorify Jesus, to comfort and console Jesus and to show Him their love by suffering with Him. To enter the fellowship of His sufferings – the Apostle Paul's desire (Philippians 3:10) – was their earnest longing. The bride yearns to share the suffering of her Bridegroom. In this way a pure virgin, a bridal soul, proves that her love for Jesus is genuine.

Furthermore, it is said that these souls in the host of 144,000 are spotless, without blemish. What an overwhelming statement to be made about these firstfruits! On their foreheads they bear the name of the Lamb – the name of the spotless Lamb. And now the same attribute is ascribed to these souls, who are consecrated to the Lamb of God; they too are called spotless. This shows that they have been conformed to the image of the Son of God – truly brothers of Jesus, who is "the first-born among many brethren" (Romans 8:29). They have been granted the grace to be transfigured into the image of Jesus. These are souls who have been made perfect, who reflect the glory and nature of Jesus.

How did they attain this glory, the privilege of reflecting Him and being the living image of Christ here on earth? Through their love for Jesus, which stemmed from ever new repentance, the sign of true humility. In this love for Jesus they were united with Him and therefore they could not tolerate the slightest sin that would grieve their Lord Jesus and prevent them from glorifying Him. Even the smallest sin immediately filled them with deep contrition. Whoever loves Jesus always has a contrite heart, for love is sensitive and quick to perceive when she has grieved the one she loves. And the penitent, the broken of heart and humble of spirit, are not only promised forgiveness, but as we can see from the Parable of the Prodigal Son, they are exalted by God, who clothes them in festal robes and puts a golden ring on their finger. No flaw can be found in them any longer.[6]

This throng standing beside the Lamb on Mount Zion has the privilege of being in the golden city. And the seal on their foreheads, the name of the Lamb and of God the Father, shines forth for all to see. In the deepest communion with the Lamb they now sing a *new* song. This is a different song from that of the singers on the sea of glass, who sing of reverence for God and total submission of the will to Him, to His ways, deeds and judgments. The 144,000 are singing a song that none can learn other than the members of this host. It is the canticle of love for Jesus, the Bridegroom. A tender, delicate song that only a bridal soul can sing of her Bridegroom, whom she ardently loves and who enthrals her heart. No one but a bridal soul can understand this song. These souls on Mount Zion cannot do otherwise than sing this song, for their hearts are filled with Jesus alone, His beauty, splendour and kingly majesty as Lord and Bridegroom.[7] Their mouths overflow with heavenly praise and they constantly seek new ways to express their love for Him.

We can almost hear the gentle strains of singing and rejoicing drifting down to us from the throne on high. It is the glorious anthem of the firstfruits, who are singing the new song to the Lamb and Bridegroom. This canticle awaits a response from hearts that are tuned to its sound and that will join in this song of a tender, fervent love for Jesus, thus bringing deep joy to His heart.

> To one name all my love belongs,
> The loveliest of names.
> 'Tis Jesus' name that fills my heart
> With rapture, wonder and delight.
> Its pure notes are a sweet refrain
> That sounds within my soul.
> His name alone is glorious.
> O Jesus mine!
>
> O Jesus, may Your name be blessed.
> You are our Love and Treasure.
> You captivate our hearts and souls;
> All that we have and are is Yours.
> And one day we shall worship You
> In heaven's joy and glory.
>
> What great rejoicing there will be!
> O Jesus, my Belovèd!
> Aflame with love Your bride will sing,
> "Hosanna, dearest Lord!" *

See *Jesus, O Joy Eternal*, LP record (songs of adoration and praise for Jesus).

As Overcomers in the City of God

And he said to me, "He who conquers shall have this heritage, and I will be his God and he shall be my son."

And in the Spirit he carried me away to a great, high mountain, and showed me the holy city Jerusalem coming down out of heaven from God, having the glory of God, its radiance like a most rare jewel, like a jasper, clear as crystal. It had a great, high wall, with twelve gates, and at the gates twelve angels, and on the gates the names of the twelve tribes of the sons of Israel were inscribed; on the east three gates, on the north three gates, on the south three gates, and on the west three gates. And the wall of the city had twelve foundations, and on them the twelve names of the twelve apostles of the Lamb. And the twelve gates were twelve pearls, each of the gates made of a single pearl, and the street of the city was pure gold, transparent as glass.

And I saw no temple in the city, for its temple is the Lord God the Almighty and the Lamb. And the city has no need of sun or moon to shine upon it, for the glory of God is its light, and its lamp is the Lamb. By its light shall the nations walk; and the kings of the earth shall bring their glory into it, and its gates shall never be shut by day – and there shall be no night there; they shall bring into it the glory and the honour of the nations. But nothing unclean shall enter it, nor any one who practises abomination or falsehood, but only those who are written in the Lamb's book of life.

Revelation 21:6 f., 10-14, 21-27

Above in the heavenly glory, as we have seen, large numbers are gathered round God and the Lamb. Each group has a different rôle, but they have one thing in common – all of them are overcomers. Overcoming is of such great significance that in Revelation Jesus challenges each of the seven churches, saying, "He that overcometh . . ." Indeed, everything depends upon their overcoming. Only as overcomers can they inherit the Kingdom of God and the crown of life and partake of Jesus' glory in the City of God for all eternity, for "he that overcometh shall inherit all things" (Revelation 21:7 av).

The throngs in the heavenly glory are called overcomers and victors, because they have waged a hard battle against Satan and sin, fighting even to the point of bloodshed. They have overcome the particular sins and bonds that Jesus pointed out to them in the messages He gave to the churches in Asia Minor:

Indifference, lukewarmness, complacency – that is, a lack of fervour in working for the Kingdom of God, a lukewarm prayer life, no spirit of sacrifice (Laodicea).

Tolerance of sin in their own lives and the lives of others, in their families, churches and surroundings – out of cowardice and fear of incurring disapproval. Conformity in order to please people (Pergamum and Thyatira).

Fear of the cross and lack of dedication to suffering (Smyrna).

The abandoning of their ardent first love for Jesus, the extinguishing of the flame of love (Ephesus).

Spiritual death, over-involvement in activities and a false kind of zeal for the Kingdom of God motivated by selfish desires rather than by Jesus (Sardis).

The overcomers fought a hard battle against sin. They came out of bitter suffering and affliction. They had to wrestle in prayer, especially during the tribulations of the end times, until they could master their fear of suffering and say, "Yes, Father" in complete dedication to suffering. Again it was the Lamb that enabled them to gain the victory. "Because he himself has suffered and been tempted, he is able to help those who are tempted" (Hebrews 2:18). They called upon Jesus as the Lamb of God and praised His precious blood that was shed for them. It broke the might of Satan, who sought to make them lose heart in suffering and temptation. There is power in the holy blood of the Lamb. This they believed. It strengthened them to battle on and endure in suffering and filled them with determination not to grow slack or lay down their arms. Thus they overcame the enemy by the blood of the Lamb (Revelation 12:11) and remained faithful unto death. And in heaven they are crowned as overcomers and victors.

Now in the end times when hell has swung its gates wide open to claim countless numbers as its prey and take them into the realm of darkness where they will be tortured, heaven has opened wide its portals to receive the overcomers as they emerge from an age that is becoming increasingly antichristian and that is fraught with trials and temptations, suffering and persecution. In His love God has prepared the most marvellous things for the overcomers.

As if dreaming, they enter a city where there is no darkness or evil to torture them, a city bathed in light, where everything is shining and radiant, a city filled with singing and rejoicing – the city of everlasting joy. No longer can their hearts be wounded or their feet cut on the sharp stones of the paths they trod in a world ruled by Satan and filled with suffering. Now their feet tread golden streets and their eyes behold palaces immersed in light. Many who once languished in dark dungeons on earth now dwell in such splendid palaces.

Those who had to flee from their persecutors in this age of misery now have a home – the golden city, which they will never have to leave. The city is surrounded by a wall of translucent, frosted-white jasper, which together with the golden streets produces a magnificent play of colours. Gates of shining pearl admit the overcomers into this city. Ever anew they are filled with wonder at all the beauty and splendour in which they now find themselves.

Did they not come from a world where everything was dark and demonic, where vulgar, diabolical music blared noisily from the radios and open windows? Now they are received by the rustling of angels' wings. Sweet and wonderful music fills the air at every movement of these celestial beings. To hear the singing of the angels and the playing of harps transports the overcomers with delight. The heavenly purity, the sonority and beauty of this magnificent music is entrancing. After traversing the streets of a sinful world, they can scarcely grasp the change. In their jobs, families and towns they had so often seen figures that filled them with grief and dismay – cold, world-weary, hardened, cruel faces marked by sin and Satan. The very sight was distressing to them. But now they are surrounded by beautiful, graceful figures emanating purity, love and joy. They cannot grasp that they may stay here with the angels and saints, never to leave this city, never to return to that diabolical world and to people who bear the characteristics of Satan.

Here in this city they are immersed in ineffable peace, which flows into them like a river of balsam. And again they cannot grasp that they may now dwell in the heavenly Jerusalem, the city of peace. Had they not lived day by day in a world rife with terrorism, hostage-taking, kidnapping, hijacking, armed robbery and murder, a world fraught with revolutions, wars and persecutions, a world engulfed in fear and suffering? But now they are in the New Jerusalem, where there is no hatred, slander, persecution, torture or murder to be found; no evil or vulgarity to be seen; no perils, fears or terrors to suffer. "Oh, that all the angels would help me to bear this overwhelming joy!" the overcomers may well cry out when they find themselves surrounded by peace – peace flowing like a river.

Such glory could have been prepared only by God, who is Love, and by Jesus, the Lamb. Indeed, His throne stands in this city – a golden and magnificent throne. There God the Father and Jesus are enthroned – but not as judges to pass judgment on the overcomers. For the overcomers had already submitted to His judgment on earth, letting His light search the depths of their souls ever anew. They had confessed their sins and washed their stained garments time and again in the blood of the Lamb. And now, much to their amazement, Jesus, whom they had loved with all their hearts and whom they had called upon in times of severe affliction to help them overcome, raises them to His throne to be at His side (Revelation 3:21). While on earth, they had borne much grief because of the sin and corruption of the nations and had prayed for them. And now as over-comers they are to rule the nations with Him. Having been humbled to the dust, treated like refuse by the Christian-haters of the end times, despised, disgraced, defamed, even persecuted and tortured, they can scarcely grasp the transfer from the deepest humiliation to the heights of exaltation. They are treated like kings by God and the Lamb, and they are led by Jesus and His angels into royal palaces, which are henceforth to be their dwelling places.

What was it that brought them such incomprehensible glory? All the suffering they had to undergo in Satan's domain on earth, where they were hated and persecuted by him. Like righteous Lot in Sodom long ago, they suffered agony in a world where drug addiction, alco-holism, sexual immorality and every kind of crime were widely prevalent. All was dark and evil about them, and their souls were filled with anguish. To their deep grief they often experienced that those who were closest to them, even their own children, succumbed to deception and chose to lead a life of sin.

But now the overcomers are bathed in a light of holiness and sinlessness; they are immersed in the radiance of pure love. Oh, what incomprehensible joy! This light comes from the Lamb, who sheds His rays upon the entire city. Indeed, the Lamb is the Light of the city. He shines a thousand times brighter than the sun. His radiance pervades everything, and the city is golden as it reflects the light issuing from the Lamb.

Joy beyond telling fills the hearts of the overcomers. What glory God has prepared for sinners for all eternity! Their wonder and amazement at such love is never-ending. In this city they will never again know hunger or thirst (Revelation 7:16), not in the spiritual sense either, for their longings for peace and communion with God are fulfilled. Now they may rest in His presence after all the battles against the forces of evil, which vented their fury in hatred and inflicted wounds upon them. Now their souls are filled with an inner peace, jubilant joy and the delight of His presence. No longer will the scorching sun beat upon them; that is, no longer will they suffer the fire of tribulation. The Lamb will lead them to the eternal springs of divine life, where they can drink their fill of peace, joy and love ever anew. We can imagine the Father now taking His child in His arms after the terrible experiences on earth during the afflictions of the end times and wiping away each tear that is still in his eyes (Revelation 7:17). Every sorrow will flee away; the overcomers will be crowned with everlasting gladness, and joy will cling to the soles of their feet, never to depart (Isaiah 35:10).[8]

Who can measure the great treasure
Suffering and grief have brought?

Who has sight and understanding
For the good that suff'ring wrought?

Only those who sowed in sorrow
And came out of deepest night
Will be crowned as kings in glory,
Shining forth in splendour bright.

Praise your suff'ring. 'Twill bring blessing,
Heav'nly joys and bliss unknown.
Let us gladly bear our crosses;
They'll bring glory at the throne.*

The Sealed Scroll and the Adoration of the Lamb

And I saw in the right hand of him who was seated on the throne a scroll written within and on the back, sealed with seven seals; and I saw a strong angel proclaiming with a loud voice, "Who is worthy to open the scroll and break its seals?" And no one in heaven or on earth or under the earth was able to open the scroll or to look into it, and I wept much that no one was found worthy to open the scroll or to look into it. Then one of the elders said to me, "Weep not; lo, the Lion of the tribe of Judah, the Root of David, has conquered, so that he can open the scroll and its seven seals."

And between the throne and the four living creatures and among the elders, I saw a Lamb standing, as though it had been slain, with seven horns and with seven eyes, which are the seven spirits of God sent out into all the earth; and he went and took the scroll from the right hand of him who was seated on the throne. And when he had taken the scroll, the four living creatures and the twenty-four elders fell down before the Lamb, each

---

* See *Well-spring of Joy* (songs of the Sisters of Mary for singing or praying), no. 257.

48

holding a harp, and with golden bowls full of incense, which are the prayers of the saints; and they sang a new song, saying, "Worthy art thou to take the scroll and to open its seals, for thou wast slain and by thy blood didst ransom men for God from every tribe and tongue and people and nation, and hast made them a kingdom and priests to our God, and they shall reign on earth."

Then I looked, and I heard around the throne and the living creatures and the elders the voice of many angels, numbering myriads of myriads and thousands of thousands, saying with a loud voice, "Worthy is the Lamb who was slain, to receive power and wealth and wisdom and might and honour and glory and blessing!" And I heard every creature in heaven and on earth and under the earth and in the sea, and all therein, saying, "To him who sits upon the throne and to the Lamb be blessing and honour and glory and might for ever and ever!" And the four living creatures said, "Amen!" and the elders fell down and worshipped.   Revelation 5

Heaven is filled with rejoicing and adoration as the overcomers worship God and the Lamb. Indeed, each of the different groups of overcomers in the heavenly glory has a special relationship to the Lamb! The innumerable multitude in Revelation 7 that came out of great affliction stand before the Lamb, the singers on the sea of glass sing the Song of the Lamb and the 144,000, the firstfruits, surround the Lamb on Mount Zion. All adoration in heaven and on earth and under the earth is accorded to Jesus as the Lamb.

This overwhelming sight during the Apostle John's vision, however, is preceded by a special event. God reveals Himself to John in majestic splendour on the highest throne, and to the amazement of all heaven He is holding a scroll in His right hand. Everyone can see that it is sealed with seven seals. When God the Father shows this scroll to all the hosts of heaven, everyone knows that the contents must be of an eternal, divine

4

and awe-inspiring nature. But it is deeply distressing that no one is able to look into it, since the Father does not remove the seals.

Suddenly, the voice of a mighty angel resounds throughout the heavenly spheres, asking, "Who is worthy to open the scroll and break its seals? Who is worthy?" At this question all the angelic hosts, the elders and the saints at the throne hold their breath. What will the answer be? They would all like to look into this scroll, most likely sensing that their eyes would then be opened to the ways of God and His eternal purposes. Above all, John must be aware of this. When this scroll is held up by God the Father for all heaven to see and the mighty angel cries out with a loud voice, asking who can open it, John knows that it is of utmost importance whether or not he is permitted to look into the scroll.

But there is no response to the angel's question, for no one is worthy to open the seals of this scroll. One must have a special right to break the seals and look into the scroll, because the contents are of such vast importance. John begins to weep. He weeps not a little, but greatly. Had not Jesus, the glorified Lord and Judge of mankind, commissioned him to write about that which is to come? For this reason John senses that he would be shown unknown things, important facts about judgments upon the world and perhaps also about God's wonderful plans for the world. All this would probably be contained in the scroll, but no one can unseal it and disclose the contents so that John could have a glimpse into the eternal purposes of God. This must be why John wept.

One of the elders in this heavenly assembly now raises his voice and says, "Weep not; lo, the Lion of the tribe of Judah, the Root of David, has conquered, so that he can open the scroll and its seven seals." Up till then John had seen only God the Father in His great majesty and glory – the almighty God whose decision that the scroll remain sealed could not be shaken. Now he suddenly sees his beloved Master as the Lamb that was slain, just as he had seen Him hanging on the cross in excruciating pain and deep anguish of soul — and yet completely different. He sees Jesus as the triumphant Lamb that has overcome and is arrayed in great power, bearing seven horns as a symbol of the perfect strength and might that enable Him to vanquish all other powers. Jesus reveals Himself as the Lamb with seven eyes symbolizing the fullness of the wisdom of God and of the Holy Spirit, who rests upon Him. His eyes search the entire earth and discern everything. He knows what the outcome of God's plans will be. Indeed, this Lamb, who had chosen to become utterly powerless, who had patiently borne all hatred and contempt and let Himself be slain by the arch-enemy — as the marks of His wounds still declare — is endowed with supreme power and strength.

What now occurs is deeply moving. All heaven is filled with awe. The Lamb comes and takes the scroll out of the right hand of Him who is seated on the throne. To his amazement John sees that, as the Lion of Judah, the slain Lamb has such might that He is able to open the seals, which no one in heaven or on earth could break because they were pressed into the scroll with divine power.

Why did not God the Father break the seals Himself? Did He not hold in His hand the scroll containing everything that would be shown in Revelation — the great, divine plan for the end times? These eternal purposes, however, have to do with the mighty battle between light and darkness when satanic forces, death, horror and sin will cover the earth to an unprecedented extent. Who then was the only One worthy to break the seals of the scroll? Only He who had fought with hell, death and the powers of darkness to the point of shedding His blood. Only He who as a lamb had innocently suffered death for the sins of others.

Indeed, Jesus has the right to fight the prince of death, the rider called Death, whose power on earth will be greater than ever in the end times. Because Jesus bears divine life in Himself, He is entitled to gain the victory not only over the forces of death operating in the end times, but over Death himself. Though completely innocent, Jesus submitted to trial four times. Consequently, He now has the right to sit in judgment and through judgment to bring to consummation the eternal purposes of God. As the spotless Lamb of God Jesus took upon Himself the sins of the whole world and shed His blood for the redemption of man. Now in this apocalyptic age He has the right and power to put an end to sin. Jesus suffered immeasurably because of the corruption of this fallen world. Therefore, He alone has the right to turn all this corruption and devastation into a new earth and to crown His redemption with the triumphant words, "Behold, I make all things new."

Indeed, Jesus' redemption will embrace all things. His redemption is not limited to individuals. God's eternal purposes, which are contained in the sealed scroll, embrace the redemption and salvation of the whole world, all nations and all living beings, and even include the creation of a new earth. This is how far-reaching Jesus' act of redemption is! God's plan of salvation will culminate in the new heaven and the new earth. All the judgments contained in the sealed scroll will lead to this goal, and all the devious schemes of Satan in the end times must serve to this end.

What a decisive moment it is, therefore, when the scroll is unsealed! All heaven is in a state of expectancy as the Lamb takes the scroll in His hand. He is able to open the seals without any difficulty. They fall off as if at the breath of His mouth, just as Jesus will destroy the Antichrist by the breath of His mouth. Jesus defeated Satan on the cross of Calvary. Therefore, at the close of the age He will put a complete end to the Antichrist and therewith to Satan, who will be thrown into the uttermost depths of hell, into the lake of fire. The meaning of the elder's words to John thus becomes evident: "Weep not; lo, the Lion of the tribe of Judah has conquered." There is no Lion to be seen, only a Lamb. But because Jesus truly became a lamb and could say of Himself, "I am gentle and lowly in heart", and because He followed His path to the end in patient, sacrificial love, He has such victorious might. This is why He is able to go forth triumphantly in the antichristian era and condemn the Antichrist to the uttermost depths of hell. Without ravaging like a lion, the Lamb nevertheless has lion-like power to accomplish all of God's purposes and to bring to fulfilment His plan of salvation.

It is of the utmost significance that Revelation always speaks of the Lamb and that in the end times the Lamb is the central figure. For the Lamb of God is the sole answer to the chaos and misery caused by the seeming victories of Satan and hell. The Lamb at the throne has opened the seals. And as surely as He has opened the seals, He will lead the world through the sufferings of the end times on to the goal of perfect glory, the new creation. If there were no Lamb of God, we too would have to weep bitterly like John — yes, we would have to despair. Although John knows that he has been redeemed, he weeps because he sees the power of sin in the world and senses that the world will perish in the havoc wreaked by sin. But then he realizes that the Lamb is opening the seals, that the Lamb is the Saviour and Redeemer of the whole world.

All heaven is filled with awe and wonder at this event. An indescribable adoration commences — no doubt the greatest ever mentioned in Scripture. First the four living creatures at the throne fall down before the Lamb, then the twenty-four elders. In their hands they are holding harps, because their words and songs do not suffice to glorify the Lamb. Mighty anthems of praise and adoration, such as no human heart could ever imagine, resound at the throne. The elders also offer incense – the prayers of the saints on earth. Thus the adoration raised here on earth is mingled with the adoration of the saints and all the angels at the throne. It is presented in golden bowls, having been removed from all its earthly imperfection.

As representatives of the royal priesthood of this earth as well as of the new heaven and new earth that is to come, the elders sing a new song. It is a song that they had not sung before. But they are able to sing it now, because they have seen that the Lamb has opened the seals and have realized that He is entitled to accomplish the marvellous purposes of God amid the chaos and misery of the end times and the seeming victories of Satan, and then to establish the new earth. This is why the elders sing a new song, "Worthy art thou to take the scroll and to open its seals, for thou wast slain and by thy blood didst ransom men for God from every tribe and tongue and people and nation, and hast made them a kingdom and priests to our God." Indeed, the ransomed form a kingdom – the new kingdom. Great and mighty is this work of the Lamb wrought by His outpoured blood! Their hearts rejoice, therefore, when they see Jesus as the Lamb – though slain, now arrayed in perfect strength and infinite wisdom – the Lamb that will lead all things to such a glorious goal.

What wonderful thoughts and plans of God the Lamb disclosed by opening the scroll! When Satan destroys, God rebuilds. Indeed, when Satan destroys Jesus' kingdom on earth, leaving nothing but a handful of persecuted and tormented believers, these, in the midst of their suffering, are being made into kings. The Kingdom of God, which Jesus brought but which He has not yet visibly established on earth, comes with them, since in their royal dignity they are representatives of the new earth. Like Jesus, their Lord and Bridegroom, they are both lamb and lion, enduring all things patiently as they suffer for their Lord; and even though they also suffer because of their sins, they are endowed with kingly authority, ennobled by their patient endurance and the wounds they bear. When Satan, the beast, manifests himself in his evil nature and dark activities on earth, it becomes all the more apparent who Jesus Christ is — the Lamb arrayed in glory, beauty and radiance, the Light of the entire City of God and, in the end, of the redeemed universe.

John now sees that the fervent adoration of Jesus, the Lamb, grows ever stronger, resounding like a mighty anthem of praise around the throne of God. Not only the elders and the overcomers cry out that Jesus alone is worthy to open the scroll. Indeed, every creature in heaven, on earth and under the earth worships the Lamb and joins in saying, "Worthy is the Lamb who was slain, to receive power and wealth and wisdom and might and honour and glory and blessing!"

Truly, the victorious Lamb is worthy of honour, for He is all-powerful, whereas Satan is actually powerless in spite of all his occult powers and his ability to work miracles. Imitating Jesus Christ and His holy miracles, Satan performs miracles, but he is completely subject to Him who crushed the head of the serpent at Calvary. At the very time when Satan rises to power and rages against the believers, he brings upon himself his final defeat, which he was destined to meet from the outset. While Satan still rages on earth and exercises his power, voices proclaim in heaven, "The kingdom of the world has become the kingdom of our Lord and of his Christ, and he shall reign for ever and ever" (Revelation 11:15). The Lamb has followed the path of enduring love to the end. The sacrifice has been completed, the victory accomplished. Therefore, Satan will meet his defeat in the end times. Jesus will establish His everlasting dominion over the earth and demonstrate His power.

How mighty is the Lord, who as the Lamb is enthroned in majesty! He rules over Satan, who has been granted power by God for only a short period in order to test man (Revelation 2:10). No other book in the Bible could more wonderfully disclose the nature of Jesus Christ than the Book of Revelation, for no other book depicts more clearly the age of terror and dread, the deceptions of Satan and the dominion of evil on earth. It shows us that while Satan rages, Jesus stands at the throne in kingly dignity and serenity, holy and unassailable. All the saints at the throne of God witness this. Though at first Satan triumphantly forges ahead in the world, his raging will only help to carry out God's plan of salvation contained in the scroll, which Jesus has already received from the hand of God. Not only does Jesus open the sealed scroll, but by virtue of His perfect sacrifice He brings to completion God's plan of salvation – a redeemed and healed world. Jesus, the patient, humbled and despised Lamb, therefore, has the right to sit on the highest throne and receive all the honour due to Him.

True, Revelation must portray the full and terrible truth about the end times – namely, that almost everyone living in the day of the Antichrist will worship him and therewith Satan. But it shows all the more triumphantly that in the end Jesus Christ, the Lamb of God – and He alone – will be worshipped from eternity to eternity. After the brief years when Satan reigns on earth and receives the homage of man, he will be hurled into the lake of fire. But the adoration of the Lamb of God will continue for ever. Yes, everlasting worship will be accorded to the Lamb. Indeed, all tribes and nations together with thousands of angelic choirs will praise and honour Him for evermore amid great jubilation.

Truly, who can compare with the Lamb! Neither in heaven nor on earth can anyone compare with Him, for He is holy and pure, a spotless Lamb. Who can compare with Him! He is Love – the patient Lamb, the Lamb that sacrificed Himself. How can we ever fathom His amazing love! Although we were His enemies and although we ever anew heap guilt upon ourselves, He lavishes His love upon us and yearns to have us with Him for ever upon His throne on high. Indeed, no one can compare with Jesus, the Lamb of God!

Who should have more reason to join in this everlasting adoration than the overcomers at the throne of God! Had they not gained the victory by the blood of the Lamb? Had they not dedicated their lives in a special way to the Lamb of God? Most of them, being believers of the end times, laid themselves on the sacrificial altar as the Lamb had done, offering up their very lives. They loved not their lives even unto death. Yet they loved their persecutors to the end. This is why they understand the Lamb of God and worship Him in a depth seldom known to believers of former times. On their path of suffering they had drawn very close to the Lamb of God.

Who can comprehend their immeasurable joy at seeing Jesus as the Lamb when they enter the heavenly glory, after having endured such suffering! If Jesus were now to reveal Himself to them as the Lord who performed great deeds, raised the dead, healed the sick and cast out demons, it would not be nearly so meaningful to them. Certainly, these were great and mighty works, but Jesus' greatest work was wrought at Calvary, where He laid

Himself on the altar and offered up His life-blood for our redemption. In this way, and this way alone, was He able to gain our salvation. Now ransomed souls come to Him as the fruit of His suffering. In times of severe affliction they experienced what it means to be redeemed by the blood of the Lamb. Redeemed, that is, set free from fear – fear of men and fear of suffering. Set free from self-centredness and all unwillingness to lose one's life. Set free from the power of Satan, who seeks to lead us astray. Set free from rebelliousness and other sins that cling to us so closely and seek to impede us. Set free by the blood of the Lamb!

Now that they have returned home as overcomers, is it not natural that they should sing and rejoice and worship the Lamb? "Glory be to the Lamb that was slain for us!" they exclaim. "Glory be to the Lamb that shed His blood for us and thus won the victory for us! Glory be to the Lamb that has made full atonement for us and led us on to the supreme goal, just as He will accomplish His purposes for mankind!" Their hearts overflowing with thanksgiving, they pay homage to the Lamb of God, and their cry of jubilation resounds ever stronger and mightier, "Glory, praise and honour be to the Lamb!"

Exultant with joy, the overcomers in heaven now praise the victory of the Lamb. The knowledge that this victory was certain gave them the courage to go the way of the Lamb with their Lord and the strength to follow it to the very end, bearing injustice, disgrace and persecution in patient love. And this way led them to the throne above. There they are united with Him, having overcome in all their suffering and struggles. They now surround us as the "cloud of witnesses" (Hebrews 12:1), the church triumphant, fighting the battle with us, who are living at the beginning of the end times. They encourage us, saying:

Gather round the Lamb today. Give Him the glory. The Lamb has won the victory. If you are wholly united with Him, you will also be victorious with Him. If you are closely knit to the Lamb on earth and choose His path of suffering and patient endurance, then you will also belong to Him above and you will be with Him in great glory for all eternity and join us and all the angelic hosts in worshipping the Lamb enthroned on high.

Join in the adoration of the Lamb. Worshipping the Lamb will protect you from the onslaughts of Satan, for there is nothing that he fears more than the Lamb, His wounds and His blood. By the blood of the Lamb Satan is defeated and put to flight. Everyone who praises the wounds of the Lamb will find refuge in them. "Honour, praise and glory be to the Lamb!" This is the triumphant anthem of praise and adoration that is being raised in heaven today in the face of Satan's activities and great display of power on earth. Make it your anthem too, for you are living in a satanic world. Join in this canticle of praise and you will be able to overcome.

> Glad choirs are rejoicing,
> God's praise alone voicing;
> All honour is giv'n to God and the Lamb.
> The heav'ns are vibrating
> With their jubilating –
> The thrice-holy anthem to God, Three in One.
>
> O honour, yes, honour
> The Lamb now be given,
> As great as the shame that He once received!
> His own now surround Him
> With honour and crown Him,
> Adoring the Godhead for evermore!*

* See O None Can Be Loved like Jesus (37 songs of love for Jesus), no. 8.

The End Times and the Wrath of God

When he opened the sixth seal, I looked, and behold, there was a great earthquake; and the sun became black as sackcloth, the full moon became like blood, and the stars of the sky fell to the earth as the fig tree sheds its winter fruit when shaken by a gale; the sky vanished like a scroll that is rolled up, and every mountain and island was removed from its place. Then the kings of the earth and the great men and the generals and the rich and the strong, and every one, slave and free, hid in the caves and among the rocks of the mountains, calling to the mountains and rocks, "Fall on us and hide us from the face of him who is seated on the throne, and from the wrath of the Lamb; for the great day of their wrath has come, and who can stand before it?"

Revelation 6:12-17

The entire book of Revelation regards the end times as the time of God's judgment and shows us a God of wrath. Cries of lamentation fill the heavens (Revelation 8:13). Thunder crashes and rumbles, lightning flashes, and powerful voices resound (Revelation 8:5). The wrath of God, which has been held back for so long, now breaks out. Time and again in the New Testament, even before the Book of Revelation, there are passages speaking of God as the Judge who expresses His wrath and executes judgment. We read verses such as the following: "It is a fearful thing to fall into the hands of the living God" (Hebrews 10:31); "Our God is a consuming fire" (Hebrews 12:29); "It is because of these things that the wrath of God comes upon the sons of disobedience" (Ephesians 5:6); "By your hard and impenitent heart you are storing up wrath for yourself on the day of wrath when God's righteous judgment will be revealed" (Romans 2:5). Jesus Himself repeatedly warns us of the terrible punishments in hell and tells us to "fear him who can destroy both soul and body in hell" (Matthew 10:28). He also declared that there would be "a terrible judgment upon this people" (Luke 21:23 NEB). And it came to pass. The city of Jerusalem was levelled to the ground and His people were dispersed among the nations.

But now the wrath of God is being poured out over the entire earth; indeed, His judgment is descending upon every single nation. The age of God's wrath has commenced. With this the time of God's grace, which demonstrated His great patience, comes to an end. In His sovereignty and might as Judge God now stands against the world, above all against the so-called Christian nations, whose sins are crying out to heaven more than the sins of the people in the days before the Great Flood. Man in general has committed outrageous blasphemy against God and exploited His forbearance, growing more and more arrogant in his derision. But now he experiences that God is the Ruler and Judge of the earth, who alone possesses power and might and who holds mankind in His hands.

Men still ridicule the "dead God", thinking that they are the rulers of the world. They derisively claim that God is powerless and pathetic and that they can treat Him as they please – if He exists at all! But now He emerges as the almighty God and Judge. People are dying by the thousand and million. Ever since men turned their backs on God, sin has been taking its toll; drug addiction and venereal disease, pollution, murder, terrorism, revolutions and wars claim their victims. As mere created beings men are subject to death and decay. God alone is everlasting. He alone is immortal, for He is the very essence of life, from whom all living things have received the breath of life. He is the Creator God, who made heaven and earth in His omnipotence, the thrice-holy God, who was, who is and who is to come.

God is alive. This is what the world is to experience now in the age of God's wrath. Alas for the man who is struck by the wrath of God, which will descend with holiness and might upon all that is proud and arrogant and that insolently raises its head against God (Isaiah 2:12 ff.)! On that day men will cry out to the mountains and rocks, "Fall on us and hide us from the face of him who is seated on the throne, and from the wrath of the Lamb" (Revelation 6:16). How terrible it will be to encounter the living God when He emerges from concealment and reveals Himself in His omnipotence and might! How terrible it will be when the wrath of God is kindled and descends upon us and our world! Indeed, people will then prefer to suffer the effects of the wrath of God by being buried alive under the rocks and mountains, rather than meet Him personally in His terrible wrath.

Yes, terrible is the wrath of God. With untold force it sweeps across the earth like a mighty gale. No one can withstand it or escape it, unless he belongs to the ransomed of the Lamb, who are spared the burning wrath of God for the sake of Jesus' blood. For the wrath of God is like a blazing fire, a mighty peal of thunder that shakes the countries of the world, a flash of lightning that strikes the earth. "His wrath is poured out like fire, and the rocks are broken asunder by him. Who can stand before his indignation? Who can endure the heat of his anger?" (Nahum 1:6). This was the cry of the Prophet Nahum. The wrath of God is a reality, as we are experiencing even now in the beginning of the end times, in the pre-antichristian era.

> The hour draws near; 'tis far away no more.
> The trumpets sound the message of the Lord:
> "The age of wrath has come!"
> The world is filled with cries of fear and woe,
> For judgment is now passed upon the souls
> Who dared to attack God.

Like flames of fire the wrath of God descends
Upon the earth, and all man's arrogance
Is turned to fear and trembling.
All those who do not humbly live today
In fear of God while yet His hand is stayed
Will be struck by His wrath.

Yes, holy, holy, holy is the Lord,
The great and mighty, everlasting God,
Who hates man's sin and pride.
So let us walk with holy trembling here,
Living each day in reverent, godly fear,
That we be spared His wrath.

The Preliminary Judgments, to Be Followed by the Judgments of Wrath

Today at the dawn of the end times God in His wrath is beginning to speak as seldom before – especially through the forces of nature. The elements are in turmoil. Today many people are learning again to tremble before the terrible God, who not only created heaven and earth, but has the wind and waves, storms and floods in His power. At His command the elements, which He created by His almighty word and which were hitherto kept within set limits, are unleashed. With ever increasing fury they sweep across the earth, wreaking havoc – and in each country differently. God is beginning to judge the earth – as was prophesied for the end times – for it has become nothing but a swamp of sin, full of crime and blasphemy, fiendish activities and Satan worship.

He rides in the storms. They are His servants – scourges which He uses to chastise the earth at the beginning of the end times. These storms and cyclones cannot be compared with the occasional natural catastrophe that struck one country or the other in former times. No, today tornadoes cut through vast districts with inconceivable force. Houses and even villages are swept away. For miles the land is laid waste and the crops are ruined. Time and again large territories are hit by recurrent storms of unprecedented violence. In many countries torrential rains flood cellars and streets; cars, houses and barns are washed away; and many lives are lost in the floods. Whenever storm clouds gather on the horizon, people begin to tremble because they have experienced the violence of previous storms and seen what damage lightning, hail and floods have caused.

On the other hand, in many places fields and meadows are being scorched by the sun during unusual heat waves. Rivers are drying up. Cattle are dying. Famine is spreading. Plagues of insects are cropping up such as the world has never seen before. Insecticides used to check them are poisoning water, air and soil. Man seeks to drive away plagues, but creates new plagues instead.[9] Earthquakes ravage large areas. Thousands are buried alive beneath buildings. Poverty, famine and disease follow in the wake of such calamities; homes and possessions are ruined. The survivors are faced with untold misery.

God has lifted up His hand; it is stretched out in wrath over the earth. The economic situation is worsening, already causing chaos to break out in many areas of life. People fear for their lives, because terrorism and violence, kidnapping, hostage-taking, hijacking, uprisings, revolutions, civil wars and thus immeasurable distress are spreading across one country after the other.

Thus the pre-antichristian era, in which we are now living, gives strong evidence that the age of God's wrath has commenced. The calamities and preliminary judgments will grow in number and proportion — but not for long. Then a world disaster, God's great judgment, will descend upon the earth.[10] But even now, in the preliminary judgments, we see that His wrath is great – as great as His mercy, forbearance and patience have been towards mankind, although their sins have reached untold proportions. The preliminary judgments will be followed by further judgments,' for the wrath of God has never been so great as in our times. Nations that had once received the message of Jesus' atoning death and used to be Christian not only reject the grace offered to them, but despise and scorn it, hating the One who made them this offer.

With the commencement of the judgments of wrath God has broken His silence. And He will speak more and more forcefully to mankind through His judgments. In Revelation we read that His voice is like the sound of many waters; thunder and lightning proceed from His throne; all heaven, the angelic hosts tremble in awe when the omnipotent, holy God begins to judge this corrupt world. His all-powerful angels have the command to execute His judgments. Indeed, they are standing ready to hurl the fire of judgment down upon the earth (Revelation 8:2-5). And now they step into action.

At God's command the four riders are beginning to tear across the earth and reap their harvest. Famine strikes one area after the other; inflation and revolutions will cause it to break out in more and more countries to an unimaginable extent. Millions are dying of starvation. Destitution and epidemics follow in the wake of natural catastrophes. Terrorism and bloodshed are constantly on the rise, instigated by an international network of organizations operating all over the world. Death will reap his harvest. Even now he has begun to set in his sickle. A nuclear war looms ahead of us; the ever-simmering conflict in the Middle East is threatening to break out into a world conflagration. Presumably, the

5

first four trumpet judgments will occur then (Revelation 8). The grass will be burnt by radio-active fallout. Springs, rivers and oceans will be contaminated by poison gas. One calamity after the other will shake the earth. The other trumpet judgments will follow. In these plagues more than one third of humanity will die — many in excruciating pain (Revelation 9).

The Two Witnesses

As soon as the antichristian dominion is established, the trumpet judgments will be followed by the outpouring of the bowls of God's wrath. But before these terrible judgments of wrath descend upon the corrupted world, an incident shows us how hard it is for God to have to judge mankind. Revelation gives us a glimpse into the heart of God. It is a heart of everlasting love — love that seeks to save souls, to help them and bring them back home to God. It is a heart that longs to bring the kingdom of heaven to men, the kingdom of happiness for which everyone yearns. Satan, the deceiver, offers them his kingdom instead. However, this can be none other than the kingdom he comes from, the kingdom of hell. And indeed, in the end times the earth has become like hell, as we read in the Book of Revelation.

But God in His love still has not given up His children. He still calls and beckons them. He yearns to draw them back to Himself. This is why He sends them the two witnesses, who are to bring them the call to repentance, the message that would open the door to the kingdom of heaven. These two witnesses appear in the first half of the antichristian era, before the Antichrist assumes complete control, and they are invested with authority by Jesus. Will mankind heed their call to repentance?

Will God be able to show grace once more rather than send His judgment of wrath? If people repent, they would see the hell in which they are living turned into heaven.

Indeed, each one of us can experience that hell is transformed into heaven. All we need to do is to turn from our sinful ways and turn to Jesus, our crucified Lord. In other words, we must repent wholeheartedly and strike a new course: for instance, we break off a bad friendship; we no longer read or look at things that excite feelings of lust in us; and if we are living in enmity or bitterness, we go to the other person and seek to be reconciled.

With a call to repentance God once more offers His children the hand of aid before the Antichrist sets up his dominion.

"... And I will grant my two witnesses power to prophesy for one thousand two hundred and sixty days, clothed in sackcloth." These are the two olive trees and the two lampstands which stand before the Lord of the earth. And if any one would harm them, fire pours from their mouth and consumes their foes; if any one would harm them, thus he is doomed to be killed. They have power to shut the sky, that no rain may fall during the days of their prophesying, and they have power over the waters to turn them into blood, and to smite the earth with every plague, as often as they desire.

And when they have finished their testimony, the beast that ascends from the bottomless pit will make war upon them and conquer them and kill them, and their dead bodies will lie in the street of the great city which is allegorically called Sodom and Egypt, where their Lord was crucified. For three days and a half men from the peoples and tribes and tongues and nations gaze at their dead bodies and refuse to let them be placed in a tomb, and those who dwell on the earth will rejoice over them and make merry and exchange presents, because these two prophets had been a torment to those who dwell on the earth.

But after the three and a half days a breath of life from God entered them, and they stood up on their feet, and great fear fell on those who saw them. Then they heard a loud voice from heaven saying to them, "Come up hither!" And in the sight of their foes they went up to heaven in a cloud. And at that hour there was a great earthquake, and a tenth of the city fell; seven thousand people were killed in the earthquake, and the rest were terrified and gave glory to the God of heaven.

The second woe has passed; behold, the third woe is soon to come.   Revelation 11:3-14

These two witnesses are God's outstretched hands imploring man, "Repent! And you will be delivered from the hell you create for yourself by indulging in your passions and by thinking you have the freedom to do what you please, no matter how sinful it is. Repent! And you will be saved from hell, which will otherwise be your eternal dwelling place." The two witnesses appear clothed in sackcloth – the symbol of lamentation, humiliation and repentance. They portray God's lament over all His children who do not want heaven, salvation, true life and everlasting joy. His children do not want the love of Jesus, who suffered death for their salvation. Instead they choose sin, hell and Satan, thus delivering themselves up to eternal torment.

Will people take to heart the words of the two witnesses when they testify to the living God? Men ridicule Him and deny His existence – will they now listen? Will they let themselves be convicted when the two witnesses proclaim Jesus Christ, who for love of us suffered death on the cross, that we might attain salvation? Will they suddenly realize with horror and shame how filthy sin has made them when they see the two witnesses from heaven, who radiate purity and light? The two witnesses come from the kingdom of light. It is their home, because they had washed their robes white in the blood of the Lamb during their earthly lives.

What must it mean for the two witnesses to have to carry out God's commission and go down to the city where once their Lord was crucified and which now, shortly before the Antichrist's reign, has become a second Sodom and Gomorrah! Had not Jesus let Himself be crucified for this city too? How His heart must grieve! His city, where He had laid down His life, has become a "Babylon of sin". Nevertheless, He dearly loves this city and sends it the two witnesses from heaven. If God could scarcely endure the thought of Nineveh's destruction, how great must be His agony to see His city deluged with sins, for they will call down divine judgment!

God grants the two witnesses great and supernatural power to perform signs and wonders, which they use to verify their testimony of Him. We can imagine all mankind watching the miracles on television and hearing the powerful testimonies about God and Jesus and the call to repentance. What an opportunity is thus given to a world sunk in sin, to people who perhaps scarcely hear or read any more about God because they have completely severed themselves from Him and because they serve sin and Satan! And now events occur that are so extraordinary and sensational that everyone's attention is gripped. The two witnesses work miracles similar to those of Moses and Elijah. They smite the earth with plagues and shut the sky, so that it does not rain. Fire pours from their mouths and consumes the foes of God. However, unlike the Satanists of today and later the false prophet, they do not perform these miracles to make a display of supernatural power before the people. As in the days of the ancient prophets their miracles are judgments and they occur whenever mankind does not heed their testimony, their call to repentance. In retrospect people have to realize that these miracles, which were the answer to their impenitence, are proof that God is alive and that He punishes both sin and the sinner. How great is the love of God in making this one last attempt to win men back to Himself before the Antichrist's reign begins!

But in response to the miracles of judgment that the two witnesses perform, the beast kills these messengers of God – although he is not permitted to do so until after they have finished their testimony. Mankind, who had heard the two witnesses' call to repentance, did not repent in spite of their testimony, in spite of their miracles. On the contrary the people are relieved to see the corpses of the witnesses lying out on the streets for three and a half days – perhaps once again on television. Indeed, they are exceedingly joyful and send each other presents in celebration of the event. No longer do they have to hear sermons on repentance. No longer are the witnesses able to smite them with the judgments of God.

O the immeasurable anguish of God! In vain had He sent His messengers. The people did not repent. The mournful words "and they did not repent" are repeated time and again in the Book of Revelation, and they reverberate throughout the heavens as the lament of God. This time God's grief is especially great, for the call to repentance was sounded in Jerusalem, His city, the centre of His beloved people, Israel, for whose sake God the Father and Jesus had suffered immeasurably.

But then it becomes evident that Satan is not stronger than the two witnesses sent by God and that God is using Satan's seeming victory to manifest who He is. He works a greater miracle still, in order to soften even the hardest of hearts and bring them to repentance. After three and a half days the breath of life enters into the two witnesses and they ascend to heaven – as Jesus did. In the same moment that the two witnesses ascend to heaven a violent earthquake occurs. One tenth of the city collapses; 7,000 perish – many of whom may have had influential positions and been responsible for leading the people astray. This time no one can say that it was a natural phenomenon like other catastrophes that occur here and there. Since it coincides with the ascension of the witnesses, everyone realizes, "This is the answer of God, because we did not accept the words of the witnesses, because we did not repent."

Now at last fear falls upon the people and they give glory to the God of heaven – especially in Jerusalem, for we hear no more of the people from the other nations, tongues and tribes, who had probably seen the corpses of the two witnesses on television. Although Jerusalem, although Israel had sunk to the level of Sodom and Gomorrah, they are His chosen people and thus the first to respond to the voice of God in judgment.

God made every effort to call His children back to Himself before the Antichrist established his dominion. He sought to prevent them from choosing the incarnate dragon as their leader, for then they would become slaves of his kingdom and soon be cast with him into the fiery lake, the place of utmost torment. The kingdom of heaven could have been theirs. So little was required of them – all they had to do was repent, turn to God, to Jesus and bring Him their sins. Then He would have blotted out their sins. Jesus would have made them a new creation if they had renounced sin and consecrated themselves to Him and to His path of discipleship. But they were not willing. The lament of God, which Jesus once pronounced over His people in deep anguish "...and you would not" (Matthew 23:37), has been sounded down through the ages – over Israel, over the nations and especially over mankind today at the beginning of the end times, in the pre-antichristian era. And it will be raised again in the time before the Antichrist begins his reign as the ruler of the whole world.

What immeasurable grief! Satan was the one they chose. Him they accepted, yes, worshipped; but God they rejected. They despised Love eternal and thus irrevocably called down upon themselves the wrath of God.

The Wrath of God Reaches Its Climax: The Bowls of the Wrath of God

I heard a loud voice from the temple telling the seven angels, "Go and pour out on the earth the seven bowls of the wrath of God."   Revelation 16:1

Now the judgment of God must be executed in all severity – in particular, upon the Harlot of Babylon, the apostate Church, and all those who joined her in offering others the fierce wine of her impure passion and who drank of it themselves. The wrath of God is kindled against the sins of immorality (Revelation 16:19; 17 and 18), for the people were unwilling to repent of them.

The wrath of God is also poured out in judgment over the antichristian kingdom. The stars are darkened and the entire kingdom is plunged into darkness. Men gnaw their tongues in anguish. An earthquake of unprecedented force causes the major cities of the earth to collapse by its terrible violence. All the islands sink into the sea. Great hailstones like heavy weights kill people and animals and ravage countries. Antichristian mankind is afflicted with torment and pain. Like a tornado the wrath of God descends upon sinful man and makes him realize what a terrible thing it is to fall into the hands of the almighty God, to experience fire and brimstone falling from heaven and the elements melting in the heat. There is no refuge from the wrath of the Lord, for even the stars are shaken and fall upon the earth.

Horror and dread rule the earth to an inconceivable degree, and people are almost crazed with fear as they speculate what terrible judgments will descend next. For the wrath of God will not cease until it has been fully vented. Since we men no longer wanted to acknowledge and accept the God of love, Jesus Christ, who was crucified for us, we must now encounter the terrible God of wrath, the Judge, and experience the reality of the prophet's cry, "Who can stand when he appears? For he is like a refiner's fire and like fullers' soap" (Malachi 3:2).

Anguished cries and moans now rise up to the God whom man had declared dead, whom he had blasphemed, ridiculed and degraded. "O what misery! What agony! O God, how terrible you are! Stop these judgments ... I can't bear it any longer ... I'm perishing in this nightmare!" The earth is engulfed in misery and distress. People shake their fists in despair against God, against this God who dares to execute such a terrible judgment and almost destroy the earth and who – so they claim – is torturing men. All of a sudden those who used to mock and degrade God and even declare Him dead, now act as if He were alive. They put the blame on Him. They call Him to account and threaten Him with clenched fists because of all the judgments that are descending upon the earth, even though they have brought them down upon themselves.

I Am God — Answer Me!

In the face of all the accusations of men – not only when the judgments of wrath reach their climax, but even now during the preliminary judgments – God, as the righteous Judge, raises a counterquestion: "Where

73

does all the terrorism come from? The civil wars? The chaos? What is the cause of the economic problems, the misery in the world, the widespread famine? Answer Me." Then they will fall silent, for in truth they have no answer. And God will give them the answer — perhaps in words like these:

"You have discarded My commandments. You have declared them invalid. In My commandments it is written, 'Thou shalt not kill.' As long as My commandments were valid, terrorism and chaos could not begin their triumphal march across the nations, nor could they tyrannize you and spread horror and dread. You are the ones who brought about this misery, which is now making you cry out in despair. Did you not glorify crime in the mass media? Did you not assign countless numbers of books with such themes to children and young people at schools and colleges and indoctrinate them with these ideas, maintaining that they are the truth? Did you not also drum into the young people that salvation is to be found in the liberation of the oppressed by guerrillas and similar organizations? In doing so, have you not made a mockery of salvation, which comes from Me alone, and brought disgrace to My path of love and humility? Have not church organizations issued the slogan throughout the world that violence in the name of 'liberation' is good and right? Did you not give millions to support the guerrillas, who, as so-called liberation movements, carried on civil wars with inhuman brutality in many countries? You are to blame, for you are the ones who propagated all these sins, which are now causing destruction and despair everywhere. You have hailed these sins as being the true ideology for freedom and have given them free rein by declaring My commandments invalid.

"You have sowed the seeds of discord between pupils and teachers, children and parents, wives and husbands

74

by abolishing the fifth and seventh commandments, which I gave to you. These you discarded in favour of anti-authoritarian behaviour and sexual permissiveness. But the systematic introduction of these evils has led to the development and rapid increase of rebellion, aggression, sexual immorality and perversion, ruined marriages and broken homes. All the moral corrosion, the disruption of the life of the family and the nation – in short, all the misery of our present times – is the result of your having discarded My commandments. They contain salvation, peace and prosperity – all of which you would have experienced if you had followed them. Yes, you have despised My commandments, which are good and holy. Even those of you who are believers are guilty of this. It was church leaders that were responsible for the disregard of My commandments and the declaration that they are no longer to be taken as valid. But because they are holy and because My name is Yea and Amen and I am faithful to My word, you must experience that every nation and every individual that does not obey My commandments incurs misfortune (Leviticus 26:14 ff.). Conversely, whoever abides by My commandments will enjoy happiness and peace – and the same applies to nations." [11]

This is probably how God would answer the questions of the many who blame Him for all the misfortunes in the world today. The truth is that sin is to blame. However, we usually do not regard sin as something horrible, something that causes destruction and terror. But because God knows and sees what sin is like, He does everything to deliver us from it. This we can see from the agonizing suffering and death of Jesus. Although He was the dearly beloved Son of God, the Father let Him suffer the horrible consequences of sin in His own body. The wrath of God that should have descended upon us in eternity because of our sins descended upon Him instead.

He suffered for our sins, so that we could partake of the grace of God.

But if we trample God's gracious offer underfoot, there is only one way left for God to set us right so that we do not have to suffer the torments of hell for eternity — and that is to judge us. It is His immeasurable anguish that prompts Him to do so. In judging us, He shows us His love, for by His judgment He prevents wickedness from developing unchecked and brings it quickly to an end. This He will also do in our times, and His judgment will correspond to the sins of mankind today, which are mounting up to heaven. Judgment such as the world has never witnessed is impending — a world disaster, which will probably be triggered off by the Third World War.

Indeed, because God is Love, He judges man. And because He is God, holy and sinless, He is still Love even when He executes judgment. But at the same time He is the righteous God, who hates sin, who judges and punishes it. This is the very proof of His love. Whether or not we are able to imagine with our limited understanding a God of wrath, who judges man, and whether or not He fits in with our concept of a God of love, God is who He is and not who we think He is. And the wrath of God is a reality — but this wrath is the anguished wrath of God, born out of His heart of love.

The wrath of God is the direct opposite of the wrath of Satan, who is the enemy of mankind. Satan's wrath is laden with hatred; his goal is to destroy everything. In his wrath and fury he seeks to bring men under his power in order to torment them. Satan rages today, because he has only a little time left to destroy individuals, peoples and countries. But when God expresses His wrath, it is to chasten and purify His children, whom He loves. He wants to help them, so that they will not be miserable for ever in the place of eternal torment. By means of judgment He seeks to pave the way for the Kingdom of God, which will bring men salvation, peace and righteousness.

Whoever does not believe that God's wrath and judgment are born out of His great fatherly love and intended for our highest good and the well-being of the world, whoever does not believe that only by means of judgment can we and the world be helped, shows that he places himself above the eternal, almighty God. Accordingly, God, who opposes the arrogant, will judge him in the time of His wrath. Whoever dares to argue with God shows that he knows nothing of the terrible nature of sin and the price Jesus had to pay for it. He shows that he does not know who God is — the holy, immortal, sublime and majestic God, endowed with glory and splendour.

O mighty, eternal, omnipotent God,
Who dares to deride Thee, Thy majesty mock?
'Tis man, who is but dust and ashes!
O mighty, eternal, omnipotent King,
Avenger of wickedness, evil and sin,
Thou art a consuming Fire!

Immortal, omnipotent Lord God on high,
Who are we before Thee? – Mere men doomed to die!
And yet we still dare to defy Thee.
What are we but clay that Thou holdest, O Lord?
If Thy love upon us in vain be outpoured,
We deserve to be dashed to pieces.

O lofty, eternal God, Lord of great might,
Our sins and our guilt are laid bare in Thy light,
Thou Judge of the world and all peoples.
O Lord, who can stand before Thee and endure?
The mighty, the arrogant and self-assured
Prevent Thee from granting them mercy.

Alas, in His presence I cannot remain!
Like lightning His holiness hurls me away;
Before Him I cannot but perish.
For I am not lowly and humble and small
Not fit for the kingdom of heaven at all;
God only gives grace to the humble.

I call now upon Thee and claim, Lord, Thy grace.
For my sake, O Lamb of God, Thou wast abased;
Thy blood blots out all my transgressions.
So I would work out my salvation henceforth
With trembling and fear, O omnipotent Lord,
E'er mindful that Thou art thrice-holy.

"Fear God!" — A Message of Hope and Deliverance in the End Times

Then I saw another angel flying in midheaven, with an eternal gospel to proclaim to those who dwell on earth, to every nation and tribe and tongue and people; and he said with a loud voice, "Fear God and give him glory, for the hour of his judgment has come; and worship him who made heaven and earth, the sea and the fountains of water." Revelation 14:6 f.

In the present day one thing is of utmost importance for us. The point is not whether we *understand* God in His wrath, but whether we can *stand* before Him when His wrath descends upon us with ever-increasing force now in the age of His wrath. Instead of asking God, "Why are You judging us so severely?", we should ask ourselves, "In what way have I so sinned that God must pour out His wrath upon us?" In the end times God is calling us, the believers, to fear Him and His terrible wrath, that is, to acknowledge our guilt before Him and humble ourselves in the dust. Only humbled souls will be spared the wrath of God; they will be able to stand in His judgment. Only such souls will be protected and delivered when judgment descends. Hence the summons for the end times, "Who shall not fear thee, O Lord ...? for thou only art holy" (Revelation 15:4 AV). Fear God! This is the divine summons for us today.

It is also the message of the angel in Revelation 14, which is addressed to all the nations in the end times – "Fear God and give him glory." This message is called a "gospel", that is to say, it is good news, since the fear of God is the prerequisite for divine aid and deliverance from the wrath of God. Thus in this terrible age of God's wrath there is a joyous message, an offer of grace for everyone who reveres God and His commandments. A gospel of significance for the end times when mankind lives in irreverence and rebellion! Never before has man's insolence been so blatant. He treats God not merely as an equal, but as a ludicrous, pathetic, despicable figure. Man's irreverence and rebellion, arrogance and self-glorification, but above all, his outrageous blasphemy cause the wrath of God to burn hot. Indeed, blasphemy is the most grievous sin, for then God Himself is attacked. Consequently, a most severe judgment will descend upon the world. However, all those who take the angel's message to heart will experience deliverance from the judgment of God.

"Fear God!" In other words: "Turn from all rebelliousness. Humble yourself in reverence before God and prostrate yourself in the dust before Him in contrition and repentance over your sins." Rebellion against God is a common sin among us believers too, although it is frequently hidden under a cloak of piety. This disguised rebellion is worse than the open rebellion of the godless. Rebellious believers ask, "Why do I have to suffer this? Why am I being led along such a hard path? Why do I have to live in this dreadful satanic age? I can't understand how You can be a God of love when You execute terrible judgments upon Your children in such wrath. Who are You, God? Do You not call Yourself a merciful, gracious God? But now You punish man so severely. Who are You, Jesus? Did You not say that You are our Saviour, that You forgive and remit sins? But now You are calling us to account for them after all."

Are we familiar with such temptations, which are usually nothing more than rebellion against God and resistance to His judgment? And do we believers not often express our rebellious thoughts against God by complaining when He remains silent and appears powerless to punish the wicked and check the advance of Satan and the moral landslide? We complain that He does not intervene and put an end to the terrorists and servants of Satan. And thus God laments, "Is there anyone among My own who still fears Me, when so many of them dare to argue with Me, the Almighty?" Yes, we dare to argue with God. If God in His great patience and forbearance is silent and defers judgment so that more souls may yet be saved, we rebel because He does not demonstrate His power. But if God then demonstrates His might and intervenes so as to prevent the earth from turning into hell and if He executes judgment so as to purify the earth out of love for His children, we accuse Him of not being kind and merciful.

We cannot afford to raise such WHYS to God – particularly today. Otherwise we too shall be overtaken by the judgment of God, which will soon descend upon the world and which without fail will also fall upon the arrogant and rebellious among the believers. This calls for repentance and a genuine about-turn. Instead of accusing God and pitying ourselves for having to experience judgment, we should lament that we cause God, our Maker, such anguish today. We should humble ourselves deeply. God offers deliverance from judgment to those who accept the atoning death of Jesus. But we, mankind today, reject His loving offer. Indeed, we spurn the love of Jesus, which constrained Him to suffer bitter death for our sakes. And thus men can no longer experience protection by the blood of Jesus when judgment descends.

Job, who did not belong to the people of God, repented of having asked God, "Why?" when he was struck by severe blows of divine chastisement. And yet he did not know Jesus, who revealed the love of God to us. Humanly speaking, when God led Job along paths of untold suffering, Job would have been justified in asking, "How can I understand God?" Then God revealed Himself to Job in His omnipotence as Creator and Lord, as we have always known Him, and addressed Job, saying, "Who is this that darkens counsel by words without knowledge? Shall a faultfinder contend with the Almighty? He who argues with God, let him answer it." At this Job replied, "Behold, I am of small account; what shall I answer thee? I lay my hand on my mouth. I have uttered what I did not understand, things too wonderful for me, which I did not know. Therefore I despise myself, and repent in dust and ashes" (Job 38:2; 40:2, 4; 42:3, 6).

Today in the age of God's wrath it is vital that we too humble ourselves before God, confess our guilt, repent of our rebelliousness and live in true godly fear. Otherwise we are lost. Today every time rebellious thoughts come, we must withstand them resolutely – for instance, by making the following testimony our own and saying in godly fear:

The wrath of God comes from His holy, loving heart and seeks to cleanse and purify His children and set them on the right path. He always has their highest good in mind.

6

Since God is good and perfect, He can do only good things for His children, even when He judges them.

The wrath of God is an expression of His ardent desire to save more souls.

However, His judgment is intended not only to set individuals right, but to purge the earth of evil-doers and pave the way for the renewal of the world.

The wrath of God is born out of immeasurable anguish, as we can see in Scripture where He so often laments that His people of the Old and New Covenant do not repent.

His wrath stems from His love for us, for only love can be so grieved to see a loved one rushing headlong into destruction by continuing to sin.

It is so hard for the God of love to judge us that He delivered up His dearly beloved Son to judgment. Indeed, in order to ransom us, He surrendered Him, the innocent Lamb, into the hands of sinners and torturers.

God does not cease to love His children even when He has to judge them.

Blessed are those who believe in the amazing patience and love of God in His judgments of wrath.

Indeed, if a person lives in the fear of God today, ever conscious of the holiness of God, who has the power to cast us into hell because of our sins, he will have a refuge when the judgment of God soon descends like a mighty gale – frightening and terrible. It is true that he will experience the holiness of God when, before the Last Judgment, the Lord judges the antichristian world, the Babylon of sin. But personally he will experience that God is a gracious Father to His children who love Him and trust Him and humble themselves before Him because of their sins. These are God's children in the truest sense of the word; they are not rebels who ask

"Why?" Rather they fear God. And they will experience the truth of that which the Prophet Nahum says, "The Lord is good, a stronghold in the day of trouble; he knows those who take refuge in him" (Nahum 1:7). Indeed, in His love, God promises to spare the God-fearing in the judgments of the end times.

"A book of remembrance was written before him of those who feared the Lord and thought on his name. 'They shall be mine, says the Lord of hosts, my special possession on the day when I act [in judgment], and I will spare them as a man spares his son who serves him. Then once more you shall distinguish between the righteous and the wicked, between one who serves God and one who does not serve him'" (Malachi 3:16 b-18).

These are the words of God, who is Love and who delights in showing grace and who suffers the utmost grief when He is forced to express His wrath and execute punishment. Everything is at stake for us, now that the age of God's wrath has come. But, "who considers the power of thy anger?" (Psalm 90:11). Whoever believes in the power of His anger and humbles himself under His judgment today will experience that God gives grace to the humble and spares them. This He will do for the believers that fear Him. They will be able to stand before God when He judges the world and when His great wrath descends upon mankind and the world like a blazing fire. And those who are still alive when the Antichrist establishes his dominion will be delivered in a wonderful way from God's final judgment of wrath upon mankind. Before this judgment descends, the rapture will take place. Jesus will take them to Himself to be with Him in His glory and thus they will be delivered out of the destruction. These souls, who fear and love God above all else, now see that the judgments and afflictions they had previously undergone have brought them the greatest blessing.

Who Will Rule the World?

In the Book of Revelation one of the major questions is: Who will rule the world? Gone are the days when any one nation was able to enjoy historical prominence, even if it had conquered a number of other nations and ruled over them. Nowadays the quest for power is on a larger scale. World control is the goal. Who will gain dominion over all the nations of the world? Contrary to all appearances, this issue will not be settled on a political level between East and West, but rather in the apocalyptic end-battle between heaven and hell. Thus the battle between the two kingdoms will be of the utmost significance.

This time it is not a question of Jesus or Satan gaining power over individuals or a particular group. In the end-time battle described in Revelation everything is at stake. Whose power will prevail over all the nations? Who will rule the world? Satan is the prince of this world; Jesus has been given all power in heaven and on earth — these are unequivocal statements of Holy Scripture. Reality, however, has proved neither that all mankind and all nations belong to Jesus, nor that they belong to Satan. The crucial moment is drawing near when that which was previously veiled to millions of eyes will be made known. The identity of the lord of all nations will be disclosed. In His divine plans God has appointed the close of the age for mankind to witness a mighty scene — the contest for world dominion.

Satan's Bid for Power

Satan's campaign has been launched. "One World" is the slogan of many top organizations in the world. This signifies that they are aiming at world control, at a unified world where even all religions will be unified and at a world government that will amalgamate all nations – in short, the solidarity of all people, nations, races and classes. The manipulators behind this move intend to carry out their plans by establishing a new ideology and a new code of ethics and by seizing power over all the nations, in fact, over the whole world. Such a course of action, however, is nothing less than a declaration of war on Jesus Christ. Although He has not yet set up His dominion over the nations, His ideology and ethics have been proclaimed to mankind and up to the present day they have wielded great influence in most parts of the world. Now Satan is offering man the antichristian ideology of his kingdom and its corresponding ethics. To this end he uses his vassals, many of whom are influential figures in the sphere of politics, high finance and religion. According to the ideology they present, the concept of a world community transcends all ethical values. The individual is required to sacrifice his private and personal views and goals – and this includes his religious convictions – in favour of those laid down by a universal society that is characterized by an antichristian spirit.[12]

Satan has been successful. This ideology of solidarity and universal equality has found acceptance. Bills designed to further this cause are already being drawn up by legislatures. In areas ranging from child care and education to religious matters this ideology is being put into practice. But these are merely preliminary steps. World dominion is the goal. The purpose is not only to indoctrinate the nations with theories, but also to make this world dominion become a reality. Satan's aspiration is the "kingdom" – the kingdoms of this world. During the Temptation of Jesus he showed our Lord all the kingdoms of the world and said, "All these I will give you, if you will fall down and worship me" (Matthew 4:9). In doing so he tempted Jesus in the very area where Jesus' primary commission lay. Jesus' heart's desire was the establishment of the "kingdom". His message was, "Repent, for the kingdom of heaven is at hand." He bade His disciples pray, "Thy kingdom come." And during the forty days after His resurrection He spoke with His disciples about the "kingdom" (Acts 1:3).

However, almost 2,000 years have since elapsed and Jesus' kingdom has not yet come. And now Satan, the adversary of Jesus Christ, is setting out to show the world in a trial of strength that he is capable of establishing the world kingdom. God is giving Satan the opportunity to emerge from the secrecy of his activities. God is allowing Satan to reveal his true nature and to show what it will be like when he sets up his world kingdom and rules the nations. Even now we can see the initial stage, because his representatives, whom he has empowered, are already coming to the fore and ruling nations. Their power is great, for Satan is Lucifer, who was probably one of the mightiest angelic princes. Although he is fallen, he is still called "the prince of this world". He imitates Jesus Christ. He wants to be like God, like Jesus, and yet cannot, because he is a mere created being, subject to God. As a rebel, he uses his power, which he still possesses, in a destructive way – hating, destroying, creating chaos, deceiving men and leading them into ruin by inciting them to lie and kill.

Satan also imitates Jesus by performing miracles. Miracles of healing have been wrought not only by the laying on of hands in the name of Jesus; there have always been instances when people possessing occult powers have produced miraculous cures by means of witchcraft and magic charms. For almost 2,000 years such activities were usually carried on in secrecy. But, today Satan has come out into the open, demonstrating his power to work miracles and making a public display of his practices. This happened, for instance, at the first World Congress on Witchcraft held in Colombia in August 1975. Indeed, the vassals of Satan in Satanist churches all over the world demonstrate the power and authority he grants to his dedicated followers. If his servants cast a spell in his name, houses burn down, aeroplanes crash, people have accidents, fall ill or even die. His power has already been manifested in innumerable satanic cults and it is gaining more and more recognition among people today. Indeed, in some places it is no longer unusual for a person to hire an adherent of Satan to cast a spell on people who make life uncomfortable for him.

Should not Satan with all his power also be able to rule the kingdoms of the world? Should not the nations submit to such a mighty ruler in fear and reverence and even worship him? His power is almost unlimited. Surely, he is capable of creating "peace and order" on earth as he promised? When he proclaimed his ideology for the establishment of his kingdom, he declared there would be equality of all nations, religions, races and classes. All authority would be abolished, for authority is said to disrupt unity, and equality is supposed to bring about peace. Consequently, people are seeking to put an end to all discrimination. For instance, in the United States powerful organizations are waging a campaign, so that "men" and "women" will no longer exist in law but only "persons". Similarly, there are no longer to be teachers and pupils, rich and poor, leaders and subordinates, and no one religion is to take precedence over others. Everyone and everything is to be equal, and this, they say, will bring about the new kingdom, the one-world superstate.

Satan will establish this kingdom. His preliminary

operations have already met with great success. His representatives, highly respected people who have a voice in the world, are beginning to carry out these plans for a one-world state. In the end Satan himself will appear and bring the plans to completion. Then for the first time it will become evident in the eyes of all that the kingdoms of this world are under one ruler. The world dominion has been set up and Satan's rule over the kingdoms of the world has been established.

This kingdom, however, is not established by a person, but rather by a beast – a beast that ascended from the abyss, from hell (Revelation 13:1). And what else can Satan bring with him but hell – the essence of all misery, terror and torment! This kingdom, which already exists underground, will be established on earth with the prince of hell reigning as the prince of the world dominion. He will step into power as the lord and ruler of the nations and all mankind – he, the liar, the destroyer, the instigator of chaos, revolts, hatred, strife and war. Today when he is ushering in his reign on earth, when there are nations already under his dominion and the ideology and laws of his kingdom are being put into practice, it is becoming quite obvious what this ruler is like. Wherever his ideology has gained a foothold and wherever he, "the murderer from the beginning", has risen to power, murder reigns over the land. Suicide. Murder of unborn human life. Murder committed even by children. Teachers fear for their lives; they are tyrannized by their pupils. The bloodshed in riots increases. General devastation heralds the ruler of the coming kingdom – Diabolus, the instigator of chaos and confusion.

Indeed, his kingdom is beginning to materialize before our very eyes. It is the kingdom of the great liar. Using clever arguments and alluring, honeyed words, he leads men astray with the slogans of unity, freedom and peace.

But wherever his kingdom has begun to be established, we find the opposite: dissension instead of unity, war instead of peace, coerced obedience instead of freedom. Families are broken up; children are taken away from their parents and become "state property"; scientists are reduced to silence; believers are persecuted. Whole nations come under the yoke of slavery and are heading for destruction.

In spite of all this, people still believe Satan, because he has power and promises them a new world. The revolutions and wars are considered to be merely a transitional stage in the establishment of this new world, the kingdom of peace and unity. But how can a kingdom of life be established by the prince of death, who spreads death and murder everywhere? How can a kingdom of unity come into existence when its founder is Diabolus, the instigator who continually causes dissension? How can a world state established by him be good and perfect when he is the Evil One, the Archfiend, who thinks and devises nothing but evil? Even now every conceivable form of wickedness and lawlessness, such as robbery, violence, murder, sexual immorality, witchcraft and blasphemy, reign over the kingdoms of the world — but how much more will they reign over the antichristian kingdom when wickedness reaches its peak! The citizens of this kingdom will live out Satan's ideology and thus manifest hell, the place their ruler has come from. The kingdom of hell will have become a reality on earth.

Whoever adopts the ideology of the prince of hell, whoever rejects authority in a spirit of anti-authoritarianism and tries to establish equality for all by forceful means, has abandoned himself to the practices of the devil. For this kind of emancipation is achieved only by rebellion, murder and violent revolutions. Those who have been deceived by this ideology are completely ignorant of the fact that they have been duped. The revolt that is supposed to create equality will result in inequality and oppression instead.

Strife, envy and hatred can never bring about a new kingdom of freedom and peace. Those who think otherwise will soon come under attack themselves; their freedom and their lives will be endangered. It is an irrefutable fact that the author of the new laws promising humanitarianism and freedom is the promoter of lawlessness. Laws and regulations in the truest sense of the words do not exist for him. The "bringer of peace" is the great warmonger, for hatred and envy can never bring about peace. He who promises unity and equality is the chief rebel, who rises up against God and every authority in order to establish himself as the sole authority and to enslave and torment mankind. Despite all this, his kingdom is beginning to be established – a fact that we can already see in a number of countries today.

Jesus Establishes His Kingdom

"Thy kingdom come," the followers of Jesus Christ have been praying down through the ages. "Why then is Satan's kingdom being established on earth?" they may ask. "Where is Your kingdom, O Lord? Did You not say that You would come again and establish Your kingdom? Have You no power, Lord? Why do You not perform miracles? Why do You not make new laws and put them into effect, so that there will be no more inequality, no more rich and poor, oppressors and oppressed, people who give commands and others who must obey them, and no more wars on earth? O Lord, how long are You going to wait before setting up Your kingdom? Do You not see that because people have waited so long in vain for the establishment of Your kingdom, they now look to the one who promises to act immediately and set up a new kingdom today?"

Many disciples of Jesus have such questions in their hearts. And perhaps Jesus would answer them in this way: "Are you waiting for *Me* to come? I am waiting for *you!* There is no need for Me to create new laws, for the law of My kingdom has already been given in the Sermon on the Mount. Live out peace instead of quarrelling and rebelling. Then My kingdom of peace will begin. Live out merciful love. Be compassionate to the poor, to the distressed and downtrodden – not, however, by means of violence and revolutions. These can never bring about the kingdom of unity. Only love can do so – love that sacrifices itself for its neighbour even if he is hostile. Give freely; then no one will suffer want in My kingdom, where love prevails – love that sacrifices itself and all that it possesses. Be meek and humble, and you will inherit the kingdom, which you are yearning for. Wherever mutual reverence and humility reign, there is no room for strife and discord. In every respect the Kingdom of God bears the opposite characteristics from the kingdom of Satan. Indeed, the very way in which the two kingdoms are established differs. Satan asserts himself with violence and hatred, and forces his ideology upon man like a dictator. But My kingdom is not a dictatorship. The kingdom of love is based on a voluntary dedication of love to live by My commandments. For I am the King of love, and I proved My love when I laid down My life on the cross for all men, so that they could become citizens of My kingdom. Just as the citizens of Satan's kingdom here on earth live, as he does, in hatred, violence and lawlessness, My citizens live according to holy, divine laws, loving God and their fellow men."

Then the disciples of Jesus may go on to ask, "But why is Your kingdom not yet visibly established over all the peoples of the earth? And why do You not assume power when we have prayed so long for this?" And Jesus may answer, "My kingdom *is* coming. It is coming in a different way from what you think, but it is definitely coming. And when it comes, it will never perish, whereas Satan's rule here on earth is brief and transient.

"My kingdom will soon be established over the whole world and every nation. The preliminary work has been accomplished. For almost 2,000 years I have been preparing the groundwork of My kingdom — that is, the host of firstfruits. Although My kingdom is not yet visible on earth and My rule has not yet been established over the nations, these faithful ones of Mine have lived according to the commandments of My kingdom in the midst of this world. Firmly established on Me, the Cornerstone, they laid the foundation of My kingdom and represented this kingdom — the kingdom of truth. They had no ulterior motives; their words were sincere; they recognized their sins and the truth about themselves. They manifested My kingdom of selfless, sacrificial love, since their lives consisted of love-inspired sacrifices for Me and the brethren. They kept nothing for themselves. Instead, like Me, they laid down their lives, gave away money and possessions, and left father and mother, home and homeland for My sake. They gave up their prestige and influence. They submitted willingly when they were deprived of their rights.

"The citizens of My coming kingdom have been invisibly paving the way for it. When the number of My small flock on earth is completed and the full measure of loving sacrifices and suffering has been reached, I shall openly establish My kingdom in the sight of the whole world. Then I shall begin My rule over the earth and the nations, together with this small, holy flock, who built My kingdom in secret."

"Oh, Lord," the impatient hearts of His disciples ask, "is this moment now near?" "Yes," He declares, "it is near. Just as the antichristian kingdom will come in the end times, as I once disclosed to My disciple John, My kingdom is about to come too. The end times have now commenced and thus Satan is on his last lap. His final attempt to assume power will be to establish his kingdom here on earth. But he will be thwarted in his ambitions, because he is doomed to eternal death in the lake of fire.

"Although Satan is extending his rule of violence and terror over the earth, this initial stage of his dominion over the nations of the world is but an indication that the time has come when I shall assume the power and kingship over the nations. Night brings forth day. The kingdom of darkness must yield before the kingdom of light, which will come when the night is at its darkest. Then the cry will resound, 'The King is coming!' In the antichristian era when the vats of sin and wickedness are full to overflowing and My forbearance and patience can no longer be extended, I shall demonstrate My power to judge sin and evil. They shall be wiped out! And the glory of My small flock will become visible to the whole world, for I shall appear with them to judge and destroy the wicked and the kingdom of wickedness."

Thus Jesus can declare, and so it will be when He comes. What then will the Evil One achieve by setting up his kingdom? His final defeat on the one hand, and, on the other, the completion and perfection of the people of God. Then the true kingdom will come – the Kingdom of God, which will remain for ever. Then Jesus will reign – He whose garment is sprinkled with blood (Revelation 19:13) and whose kingdom is built on sacrificial love that sheds its blood for others. He will reign as the One called Faithful and True. Indeed, then it will become evident that He has made His promise come true. He has led His flock through persecution and untold suffering on to the supreme goal of perfection. He did not abandon His world and the nations to Satan; Satan was only permitted to test men, just as gold is tried in the fire. In actual fact everything works towards the coming of Jesus' kingdom.

And this kingdom will come. The hour will dawn when His flock no longer needs to pray, "Thy kingdom come." Instead they say, "Behold, it has come. The King of kings has begun to reign." His kingdom is now established on earth. The words, "*Thine* is the kingdom and the power and the glory" have come true. The kingdom of Satan has fallen and Jesus' kingdom is established. He has begun His reign. No human words can describe what the rule of the Sovereign, Jesus Christ, is like!

The word "redemption" is written in bright shining letters on the gates of the kingdom of Jesus, the Redeemer of mankind. For the words of Scripture have come true, "The former things have passed away . . . Behold, I make all things new." A new kingdom now arises in place of the kingdom of hatred, violence and war. This new kingdom is a kingdom of peace, for Jesus is the King of peace. Accordingly, the nations "shall beat their swords into ploughshares, and their spears into pruning hooks; nation shall not lift up sword against nation, neither shall they learn war any more" (Isaiah 2:4). It will be possible to live in security, for as the Lord says, "My people will abide in a peaceful habitation, in secure dwellings, and in quiet resting places" (Isaiah 32:18). The bow, the sword and the spear are broken, as was promised, so that everyone can live without fear. Peace will spread out over the animal world as well. "The wolf shall dwell with the lamb, and the leopard shall lie down with the kid" (Isaiah 11:6). The plant world too, indeed, the entire earth will partake of the blessed liberty that comes with the redemption of

God's children. And the reason for this peace will be that the people have "a Fountain to cleanse them from all their sins and uncleanness" (Zechariah 13:1 *The Living Bible*). For the people that dwell in this kingdom will be forgiven their iniquity (Isaiah 33:24).

In awe we worship God for the mighty purposes and plans that He has for the whole world, plans that He has borne in His heart of great love from the beginning of time. His goal since ages past has been the Kingdom of God, the kingdom of true peace and joy.

Righteousness also dwells in this kingdom, for Jesus is the King of righteousness. Injustice and lawlessness exist no longer, for the man of lawlessness has been destroyed. Violence has disappeared from the land; devastation and destruction have ceased to be. There are no more thieves, robbers and murderers, no more liars and deceivers. Sin has been vanquished. The commandments of Jesus are now binding for one and all. Everyone abides by them. The time has come when, as Scripture says, all men live in the fear of the Lord because the law of God is written upon their hearts (Jeremiah 31:33).

Indeed, the King, who is eternal Love, has established His kingdom, in which love reigns. Everything in His kingdom is characterized by the royal laws of love – a love that lasts for ever. Everything is permeated by divine harmony, abundance and fullness of life, which flow forth into all the world. In previous ages only individual members of Christian nations had a living faith in God and were a testimony of love by their lives, but now all the nations are converted to the Lord. For as it is written: "All the ends of the earth shall see the salvation of our God" (Isaiah 52:10); "All the ends of the earth shall remember and turn to the Lord; and all the families of the nations shall worship before him" (Psalm 22:27). Man will serve God and his fellow men according to the commandment of love. True unity and harmony will reign.

This Kingdom of God where peace and joy, righteousness and love dwell, a kingdom described in many prophetic passages, will begin on earth after the returning Lord has defeated Satan and bound him (Revelation 20:2). But at a later point heaven will actually come down upon the earth; the City of God will descend and the new earth will come into being (Revelation 21:1-4). Gladness, rejoicing and festal songs will fill the New Jerusalem and its glory will be beyond compare. "The city has no need of sun or moon to shine upon it, for the glory of God is its light, and its lamp is the Lamb" (Revelation 21:23). Indeed, it has come true: "The kingdom of the world has become the kingdom of our Lord and of his Christ, and he shall reign for ever and ever" (Revelation 11:15).

A Challenge to War —
The Beast's Army Is on the March

And the fifth angel blew his trumpet, and I saw a star
fallen from heaven to earth, and he was given the key
of the shaft of the bottomless pit; he opened the shaft
of the bottomless pit, and from the shaft rose smoke like
the smoke of a great furnace, and the sun and the air
were darkened with the smoke from the shaft. Then
from the smoke came locusts on the earth, and they were
given power like the power of scorpions of the earth ...
They had scales like iron breastplates, and the noise of
their wings was like the noise of many chariots with
horses rushing into battle. They have as king over them
the angel of the bottomless pit; his name in Hebrew is
Abaddon, and in Greek he is called Apollyon.

Revelation 9:1-3, 9, 11

A mighty conflict is taking place between the two kingdoms now at the close of the age. To use an illustration:
Two hostile armies representing two different kingdoms
march out to war. They issue their front line reports.
First one side appears to be winning, then the other. The
victories proclaimed by the one army are surpassed by
those of the other. However, intermediary reports are
not decisive — this we learnt in the Second World War.
The point is which side will emerge victorious from the
final battle and who will have the last word to say at
the end of the war.

In the last stage of God's plan of salvation two armies
are setting out to war to gain dominion over mankind
and the kingdoms of this world. In Revelation 9 we read
that the army of demons launches an offensive. They
come into the open, emerging from the kingdom of hell,
where they had been locked up as in a dungeon. A
world-shaking event! — the gates of hell are thrust open
and the powers of darkness are unleashed. With un-
restrained fury and malice the demonic forces — just

7

waiting for this moment – now fall upon mankind. For thousands of years they had been held captive in their kingdom, in the shaft of the bottomless pit (Revelation 9:1). As it is written, "God did not spare the angels when they sinned, but cast them into hell and committed them to pits of nether gloom" (2 Peter 2:4). Formerly angels of light like Lucifer, they had dwelt in the kingdom of darkness ever since their fall. Jesus had the key to this pit – they could not break loose. Only Satan would time and again traverse the earth with a small band of demons, for as the Bible says, "We are not fighting against people made of flesh and blood, but against persons without bodies – the evil rulers of the unseen world, those mighty satanic beings and great evil princes of darkness who rule this world" (Ephesians 6:12 *The Living Bible*).

Now God's moment has come to open the bottomless pit. "Woe!" cries the angel, for nothing is more dreadful than when the sealed gate of hell is opened and all the demons are let loose. But this can only happen, because it is permitted by the Lord of lords, God Himself, to whom the demons also are subject. The eternal God gives the angel the key to open the bottomless pit. Thus it is opened at the bidding of God, who has the keys of Death and Hades. By giving the angel the key, God ultimately gives Satan the command, "Come out of hiding and show the power and might that is given to you on earth." Yes, this power was given to him by God (Revelation 6:1 ff.) – but only for the purpose of separating the chaff from the wheat.

The army of Satan surges out and swarms over the earth under its leader, the angel of the bottomless pit (Revelation 9:11). Mighty representatives of this kingdom swiftly mount their steeds, confident of victory. Very likely they are princes of this kingdom, the kingdom of darkness, for one of them is Death, the ruler of the realm of the dead. His power is so great that he will be the last foe to be vanquished. The entire realm of the dead forms his retinue (Revelation 6:8). Other commanders of the kingdom of hell mount their steeds (Revelation 6:3-6). These are the satanic princes in charge of war and famine. They race across the earth, knowing that the moment has come for them to seize power and establish their dominion over the whole world. The rider on the white horse sets out, certain of victory. He knows that his arrows will hit the mark, that he will conquer one country after the other and bring the people under his satanic rule, enslaving them in body, soul and spirit.

Lastly, Satan himself, the beast from the abyss, will appear, after the riders and the army of demons have done the preliminary work. Their task was to cause devastation and misery by means of wars, revolutions, famine and other afflictions, but above all to poison and cloud the minds of men. Clouds of smoke precede this army of demons, which falls upon men in a frenzy (Revelation 9:2). Just as today pollution causes a poisonous cloud to settle suddenly upon a district and envelop it in a fog, so the open abyss of hell emits a cloud of smoke charged with poison that contaminates the people, puts them in a stupor and induces them to shed inhibitions and indulge in all manner of evil pursuits. Almost imperceptibly they are indoctrinated with everything that appeals to the fallen nature of man, whose arrogant, rebellious heart craves for freedom from all authority and from every kind of cross. The hellish vapour of the new ideology is used to cloud their minds, so that they will go over to the army of darkness.

On the other side are the adherents of the kingdom of light. A mortal combat commences. The kingdom of righteousness and truth, peace and love versus the kingdom of unrighteousness, falsehood, war and hatred. As if in a delirium hell rages to conquer men. A number of demons attack each person, fighting fiercely to take him as their prey. Only if a person is equally fierce in his battle against them, can he escape their clutches.

But generally speaking the battles that are waged seem to be one-sided. Satan conquers one soul, one nation and one part of the world after the other without much opposition, as if the kingdom of light, which is under Jesus, the Prince of life, had no power. Thus the white rider, whose deceptive appearance suggests that he brings people true happiness when actually he brings them misery and destruction, proceeds from victory to victory, meeting scarcely any resistance.

It is as if the kingdom of Jesus Christ and its army have fallen asleep and are not capable of opposing this mighty victor. Almost effortlessly he prevails in the realm of law and morals. Whenever his arrow, which has the same effect as the drug addict's needle, hits a nation, time-honoured laws that were based on the commandments of God are changed; penal laws prohibiting abortion, blasphemy, pornography, homosexuality are discarded; grave offences are no longer punishable by law. People are "freed" from authority, from regulations and laws. The institution of marriage is regarded as outdated. "Liberated" from the commandments of God and the voice of conscience, man loses his foothold; he is free to indulge in all manner of wickedness and is thus a slave of Satan. A diabolical atmosphere is spreading. People are becoming more and more like citizens of a satanic kingdom. Small groups still offer resistance; they are still able to check Satan's victorious advance somewhat, although they cannot prevent it.

The antichristian army marches under a certain banner, the standard of the beast, whose appearance is terrible and dreadful. He is exceedingly strong and has huge iron teeth and bronze claws. He crushes and devours and tramples under foot what remains. And his mouth is full of boasts. He flings truth to the ground; in all that he does he succeeds. He aspires to be as great as the host of heaven, that is, the angels (Daniel 7:7, 19, 20; 8:10-12).

The beast's soldiers hold their standard high, confident of victory and convinced that soon all men will be united under this banner. For we are living in an age of internationalism when there is a strong move towards unification. These soldiers march on in the assurance that they will proceed from victory to victory, because their commanders have "huge iron teeth and bronze claws". They are strong, for they have chosen violence and revolution as their confederates, trampling under foot everyone who refuses to be re-educated and join the ranks of the revolutionaries. Ruthless violence is written on their banner. And under this banner they will establish a so-called kingdom of peace, where everyone will be united under one ruler and placed on the same level with everyone else. Their weapons match their banner; they are incredibly strong, relentlessly crushing everything that stands in their way.

The coming of the terrible beast is prophesied for the end times. And there are many indications that everything we read about the beast of the abyss in Revelation 13 can soon become a reality. Indeed, modern technology has already provided the necessary requirements for world government to be effectively carried out, although this once seemed impossible. A computer system, for instance, would enable the Antichrist to exercise complete control over his world dominion.

As early as 1970 Anton LaVey, the High Priest of the Church of Satan in the United States, declared that Satanism would lead to a world police state under a totalitarian government. And it is a known fact that Satanism is working together with other international organizations that are of an antichristian spirit. Thus we can see that the army setting out to war under the standard of the beast plays a highly significant rôle in the end times. The fate of mankind and the whole world will depend upon whether this army gains the victory. Well-organized, it advances with clear marching orders. Satan's aim is to gain power over the whole world in order to establish the new kingdom. When he appears as the Antichrist and sets up the antichristian kingdom, it will seem as though he has succeeded in attaining his objective once and for all.

Elated by his mighty conquests, Satan then plans to celebrate his greatest victory in the sight of all the world and deliver the death-blow to Jesus Himself. In blind presumption, the Antichrist with millions of soldiers from his world dominion will challenge Jesus, the Lord of the rival kingdom to the final battle at Armageddon. There he intends to make the greatest display of his power by staging miracles in the sight of the whole world. His objective is to prove that he is the final victor over the whole world. However, this moment has not yet come. The battles are still being waged.

Yet it is a strange war that is taking place. We do not see two equally matched sides facing each other. The one is exceedingly powerful, knowing nothing but victory, whereas the other yields, offering almost no resistance. Indeed, large numbers that once belonged to the Kingdom of God even open their doors to the enemy when he sends out his agents to cloud the minds of men. They believe his deceptive offers of peace and happiness. Instead of fighting against him, they let him continue to gain power and they even support him. Consequently, he grows more and more confident of victory, increases his might and is able to secure his position in one country after the other.

Only one stronghold offers him iron-like resistance.

This bastion is comprised of a poor, small band of souls – the followers of Jesus of Nazareth, the crucified Lord. They follow Him along His path. As loyal citizens of the Kingdom of God they faithfully cling to the laws that Jesus gave for His kingdom and fight to the point of bloodshed against the advance of the rider on the white horse. They expose his deceptions, raise their voices in warning, challenging others to break with him and his teachings and to join forces wherever they are so as to form a small army and fight under the banner of light. Whenever the prince of the kingdom of darkness seeks to invade new territory by means of lawlessness and blasphemy, they are on the alert. They do everything within their means to check the enemy by erecting a wall of powerful and fervent prayer, by the testimony of their words and lives, and by issuing warnings in order to help men in their confusion. Yet generally speaking, they experience nothing but defeat. Almost daily the enemy advances further, winning more supporters and influence in an increasing number of countries. He introduces his teachings and standards even before his reign is openly established in the antichristian kingdom.

Thus it really does appear as though this battle will end in victory for the prince of darkness. Even today the facts point to this. Man is in the process of founding a world superstate. And when this is achieved, the small resistance groups that fight for the kingdom of light and still dare to oppose the advance of the rider on the white horse will be put to death. For almost the whole world will have accepted him. The solution to the "Christian problem" will be the annihilation of the small band of followers, and thus the fate of Jesus Christ's kingdom is sealed – or so it appears. The prince of darkness marches on towards the final triumph, confident of victory; for when the Church of Jesus has been wiped out, the last resistance will have been broken.

The Victory of the Lamb and the Martyrs under His Banner

However, in his attempt to gain the final victory, Satan makes one mistake in his calculations. By attacking and destroying the small flock, the holy remnant made up of those who remain loyal to Jesus Christ and His commandments, he thinks that he is removing the last opposition to his world dominion. But he does not consider what consequences it will have for him when he sheds the blood of the saints. By spilling innocent blood, Satan creates martyrs. And martyrs have always been the seeds of the Kingdom of God; they cause it to flourish. This manner of death yields eternal, divine life. Satan, blinded by rage, does not realize that there is power in suffering.[13]

Like the vast army of the beast, the small army, which seems so ludicrous to Satan, also marches under a standard that is indicative of its weapons. On this standard a symbol can be seen bearing the opposite characteristics of the beast – the image of the Lamb! In contrast to the beast, whose appearance is terrible and frightening, the Lamb's appearance is heart-moving. He is wounded, and from His wounds blood is flowing. He lies there, surrendered to all the suffering and to all the malice that others vent on Him, the innocent Lamb. He sheds His blood for others, whereas the beast sheds the blood of all his victims, whom he crushes with his teeth of iron. The Lamb of God, who suffers for the wickedness of man, gazes lovingly at His tormentors and lets Himself be slain for their sakes. He loves the sons of men. This sacrificial love, exemplified by Jesus, is the banner of victory under which the army of the Lamb advances as it fights to gain the victory for Him.

But how does this handful of soldiers in the Lamb's army intend to overcome the enormous army of the beast and its commanders? Their course of action is clearly outlined; their weapons are evident. They do not have iron teeth and do not wildly bite everything in sight, ravaging towns and countries; nor do they have claws of bronze to crush people. Their weapon is the gently flowing blood of the Lamb, for streams of blood flow forth from them too. In their battles they do not inflict wounds; rather they let wounds be inflicted upon them. But will this not inevitably lead to the defeat of Jesus' army? Will this not pave the way for the victory of the beast? No, the beast will be overcome by the blood of the Lamb, which the followers of Jesus praise and claim. Their faith in the victorious power of the blood of the Lamb is their shield against the attacks of the army led by the beast. And authority is granted to them, because in the power of the blood of the Lamb they are ready to shed their blood for their beloved Lord.

This small army marching under the banner of the Lamb is thus prepared to offer the beast its own blood. In Revelation 12 we read that the martyrs "loved not their lives even unto death". Yet by their death they defeat the raging beast, who ruthlessly kills all that stand in his way as he sets up his kingdom. Martyrdom for Jesus' sake brings victory, life and resurrection. Victory is contained in an innocent death for the sake of others. Martyrs are the most dangerous enemies for the army of the beast. Their weapons strike without fail and in the end they will give the beast's army the death-blow.

Who is it then that is marching today against the army of the beast, which is fanatically fighting for the establishment of his kingdom? It is the army of martyrs. These are souls who are prepared to face death – resolute souls, ready to lay down their lives for their Lord, the Lamb of God, whose banner they hold high. They know that the victory belongs to Him. Once long ago at Calvary the death-blow was dealt to Him by the same foe, who is now manifest as the beast. Yet in actual fact it was Satan who received the death-blow. Jesus rose from the grave on the third day, arrayed in glory and power. Death was vanquished and Jesus established His kingdom in its first stage together with His picked troops, His true disciples. These were the firstfruits of the Early Church, who were prepared to enter suffering and death for the sake of their testimony to Him.

Those who belong to their number today are prepared to fight, together with Jesus, until the final victory is accomplished and Jesus sets up His dominion over all nations. They know that the victory belongs to the small army of the Lamb and not to the vast army of the adversary. Fearing nothing, they continue to bear testimony to Jesus Christ, the King who will come again. They sacrifice their lives for Him, since they do not love themselves, but rather Jesus, their Lord and Bridegroom. The other side is no match for such love, for this love is "strong as death" (Song of Solomon 8:6).

Even if the commanders of the beast's army and his soldiers furiously seek to wipe out the army of the Lamb today, it is of no avail, for they will only destroy themselves by opposing the will of God and His divine laws. Jesus says, "He who believes in me, though he die, yet shall he live" (John 11:25). Because the divine life pulsating through the army of the Lamb is eternal life, it can never be killed. This divine life, which is fed by love for Jesus and the Father, is immortal like Jesus Himself, who is the very essence of life. Thus the mortal army of the beast is fighting against an immortal army that can never be wiped out because life that comes from God is victorious over death and hell.

This reality has often been demonstrated in countries that are already under the dominion of the beast. The more the waves of atheistic hatred and violence rolled over the believers, the more this imperishable life spread in these countries. The army of the Lamb grew, and revivals broke out.

In the final battle against the beast, which is being fought on a worldwide level, an all-out effort is required. All those who belong to the army of Jesus are challenged to enter warfare under the one banner that will bring them victory – the banner of the Lamb. Today only those believers who uncompromisingly stand beneath the banner of Jesus, just as the soldiers of the rival army stand beneath theirs, can be victorious and help to achieve the victory for Jesus' cause. The followers of the beast know what they want and what they have chosen – the way of violence and aggression. Whoever belongs to them must be able to kill. But those who wish to belong to the army of Jesus Christ and to march beneath His standard must be able to lay down their lives and must have really chosen the way of the Lamb.

In practice this means walking in patient endurance and silently bearing injustice and affliction in everyday life at home and at work. Otherwise we have no power as soldiers of Jesus Christ; for when the sins of rebelliousness, self-assertion, quarrelsomeness and hatred cling to us, and when we lash out at others in anger and bitterness, we resemble the beast and not the Lamb. Sin weakens us. It enslaves us. It brings us under the yoke of bondage. Then we are not able to fight for Jesus in His army and to oppose the beast; for only if we have the nature of the Lamb, can we conquer the beast. Otherwise we are strengthening the beast, the enemy of Jesus Christ's army, and stabbing Jesus in the back. It was as the Lamb that Jesus overcame Satan. And when Jesus is depicted in His majesty and glory, it is as the Lamb. Only the nature of the Lamb, the spirit of self-sacrificial love that pours out its life-blood for the sake of others, leads to victory. The victory belongs to love and not to hatred. For God is Love, and love, like God, is immortal. It is never-ending (1 Corinthians 13:8), and for this reason it alone has true power. The beast, however, and hatred are mortal; they will come to an end; they are doomed to die. The beast, Satan, is a created being and will suffer judgment.

Now with the beginning of the end times the watchword is, "Rally round the standard of the Lamb that was slain, the victorious Lamb." Whoever does not march under this standard is lost. He will experience nothing but defeat in the battle with the army of darkness. If the other side detects characteristics of the beast in us, we give the army of the beast an opportunity to attack and defeat us at these weak points. Then the palm of victory will not be granted to us. And whoever does not win the victory in the final battle will be defeated for ever. Only those who march under the standard of the Lamb, that is, who have chosen the way of the Lamb as their way, will be victorious. These are they who set out for battle with the motto, "Follow the Lamb wherever He goes." Once again today the Lamb of God goes on ahead of us, the army of His disciples, who follow Him into suffering and death because they love Him.

We are living in an age of martyrs. When the Bible speaks of the beast, it also speaks of the martyrs. The beast and the martyrs belong to the same era. And just as the beast is already present among us in the person of the commanders of his army, the age of martyrs has also dawned. During the last few decades in the atheistic, communistic countries alone there have been more martyrs than in all previous centuries taken together. Many millions have been killed. Hated, persecuted in all nations, everywhere in the world! — these words are becoming an ever-increasing reality (cf. Matthew 24:9). For, "I had seen this horn warring against God's people and winning ... He will defy the Most High God, and wear down the saints with persecution" (Daniel 7:21, 25 *The Living Bible*). He "was allowed to make war on the saints" (Revelation 13:7). "Men have shed the blood of saints and prophets" (Revelation 16:6). "I saw the woman [the harlot on the beast], drunk with the blood of the saints and the blood of the martyrs of Jesus" (Revelation 17:6).

The end times – the age of martyrs! History repeats itself. The present age can be likened to the days of the Early Church. We see Jesus Christ's band of soldiers entering battle, prepared to lay down their lives for Him and His kingdom. Bearing the mark of the Lamb, they are living crosses – consecrated to the Lamb, the Cross-bearer and crucified Lord. They are ready not only to bear their cross after Him in complete dedication to suffering, but out of love for their Lord to lay down their lives – and perhaps even be crucified as He was.

What mightier soldiers could there be than those whose dedication to suffering is based on a personal relationship of love and thanksgiving to the Lamb of God, the Lord who was crucified for them! Their love makes this army strong and invincible. "But", we may ask, "can this also be true when Scripture says that the beast 'was allowed to make war on the saints and to conquer them'?" Yes, even then. True, they will be conquered – but not overcome, for they will be victorious in the final battle. What a triumphant assurance! – the victory belongs to the Lamb and thus to them. At the Battle of Armageddon Jesus will once again come from heaven as the mighty Victor. Then the situation will be reversed. It will not be the beast who defeats the saints, but the Lamb who defeats the armies of the Antichrist, for the Lamb is the Lord of lords and King of kings. Jesus will appear and win the victory with His followers – the called, the chosen, the faithful (Revelation 17:14) – who have been killed by Satan, but raised to life by Jesus.

Here too, it is the faithful who are at the side of the victorious Lamb. They had remained faithful to Jesus unto death, whereas all the others had fallen away from Him. They stayed at Jesus' side, while Satan, the ruler of the rival kingdom, reigned over everyone and everything, and while Jesus was despised, degraded and hated as once long ago, but this time by all nations. These are Jesus' loyal soldiers, who fought for His kingdom when it cost them blood and tears. These are His chosen ones, who let their election be tried and tested in the furnace of affliction when God remained silent and gave the enemy power to torture and kill them, yes, to prevail over them throughout the world. But when they emerged from the fiery furnace, they were like refined gold and invincible for Satan. Having been tested in suffering and trials of faith, they proved their loyalty. As partners with Jesus in war and now also in victory, they are at His side when He vanquishes Satan and his kingdom. Now the beast is captured and with him the false prophet, and both are thrown alive into the lake of fire (Revelation 19:20).

What an amazing fact! – the ravening wolf was put to death by the Lamb that poured out His life-blood. This is now made manifest in the sight of the whole world. By virtue of His sacrificial love the Lamb has become the Prince of victory, the triumphant Lamb, for eternity. And everyone who fought under His standard and bore the image and nature of the Lamb experiences that "the kingdom and the dominion and the greatness of the kingdoms under the whole heaven shall be given to the people of the saints of the Most High" (Daniel 7:27).

Dedication to Suffering Enables Us to Suffer

The soldiers of Jesus Christ in the army of the Lamb are strong in faith. They believe in the victory of Jesus, which will come without fail. They know that their Lord will come into His dominion over all the kingdoms of the world and that they will rule with Him. They reckon with the fact that when the beast tortures them and seems to crush them with his feet, Jesus will be with them and let them experience the tremendous power of His love. They know He will prove that He is mightier than the enemy. He will impart to them a measure of His great power to endure suffering, so that they can testify, "I can do all things in him who strengthens me" (Philippians 4:13). They believe in His faithfulness and trust that their Commander, the Lamb, will not forsake them when the moment comes for them to sacrifice their lives for Him, but will lay His right hand upon them and say, "Fear not, for I am with you ... I will strengthen you" (Isaiah 41:10).

Because they live in the age of the beast, they have counted the cost and committed themselves beforehand to bear suffering and torture for Jesus' sake, out of love and thanksgiving to Him. By repeating their dedication to suffering ever anew, they grow in strength and become more and more capable of entering the sufferings of persecution – cross-examinations, brainwashing, imprisonment and labour camps – even if it should cost them their lives. They know that Jesus is with them. They know that no matter how great the suffering and torment may be, their Helper and His love are greater still. Indeed, God is always greater.

Now as long as they are still free, they have but one plea:

Lord Jesus,

Strengthen my faith; let it be strong enough to meet the affliction that awaits me. Deepen my trust in the goodness of the Father, who never lets His child be tempted beyond his strength. Let my love for You, Lord Jesus, become so deep and strong that I cannot do otherwise but suffer for You out of love. Let me suffer to Your glory and because of Your grief over all the hatred and blasphemy heaped upon You today. I want to suffer out of gratitude that You have saved me from the jaws of the beast for eternity and transferred me to Your kingdom. Let me suffer, so that Your kingdom can come soon.

Take my life, Lord Jesus. And though my heart may break – especially if I must see my dear ones entering torment – I want to follow You, the Lamb, wherever You go and wherever You lead me. I have committed myself to following Your pathway, which will end in heaven where You are. There I shall receive the palm of victory and the crown of glory and be united with You for ever at Your throne. Amen

If this is our plea, we are members of the army of the Lamb, to whom the victory belongs and for whom the crown is laid up. Today, in the end-time battle it is worth being in the army of the Lamb and fighting on His side, dedicated to all suffering and prepared even to sacrifice our lives. For whoever follows Jesus, the victorious Lamb, attains victory and eternal life. This life is the one true reality and it will never perish, unlike the kingdom of the beast, whose fate has already been sealed. Indeed, as kings and priests, these followers of Jesus will partake of the one eternal, everlasting kingdom.

Short Prayers for the Time of Persecution

Grant me faith.

Grant me the desire to suffer for You.

Give me a courageous heart.

Set me free from my ego.

Deliver me from fear.

Let me be wholly united with You.

Let heaven come down.

O Jesus, be close to me.

Strengthen me by Your blood.

Give me a faith that moves mountains.

Give me the strength to lay down my life.

Help me to say, "Yes, Father"

Let me stand firm.

Let me lift up my eyes to You.

Let Your peace descend upon me.

Let Your love flow into my heart.

Give me the strength to make sacrifices.

Give me the strength to suffer.

Let me behold You as the Man of Sorrows.

Let me be a living testimony to You.

Let me rejoice, saying, "Soon I shall be home in heaven."

Let me believe that You will be with me.

Let me believe that nothing can separate me from You.

Let me believe that Your aid will come.

The "Male Child" Caught Up
to the Throne of God

The fact that God's own are persecuted and hated, degraded and tortured today in body, soul and spirit is — in spite of all the suffering — like a triumphant flourish of trumpets announcing, "The King is coming; the Bridegroom is coming. Prepare yourselves!" Just as the earth is thoroughly polluted by sin and evil, rife with hatred and persecution of the elect, whose blood is spilt upon the earth, it is also true that the return of the great King is at hand. Jesus is coming again soon! This fanfare is especially meant for those who are called to take part in the rapture. During the time of persecution they will be protected, Something wonderful awaits them: when their Bridegroom appears, they will be caught up to meet Him in the air.

"She brought forth a male child, one who is to rule all the nations with a rod of iron, but her child was caught up to God and to his throne" (Revelation 12:5).

All over the world the Lord is preparing this group, which He has destined for the rapture. During the time of persecution they will be protected — perhaps in places of refuge — and thus spared a martyr's death. But to remain alive on this hell-like earth means immeasurable anguish, martyrdom of soul and spirit for these believers. It also involves physical suffering to some extent, because they share the afflictions of the beginning antichristian era.

On all sides they are closed in by darkness. Sin has left its dreadful imprint on the people about them. Hell-like laws and evil modes of behaviour govern the atmosphere. In addition, they must witness how believers with whom they were closely knit in the love of Christ are tortured, yes, even killed. They hear the anguished cries of the tortured, but are unable to help them. Moreover, they themselves are constantly being pursued by fiendish agents who seek to track them down and find their hiding places in order to kill them like their brothers. They live in fear and trembling, deprived of food and clothing – hated, despised, ever in danger of being betrayed into the hands of their enemies. One betrayal after the other is committed by brothers who used to sit with them at the same table and who now hand over their fellow-believers to the executioners. The flames of affliction mount ever higher. And though this group experiences protection, their place of refuge is a place of tears.

The servants of Satan think that they can now officially establish the kingdom of their master as a world dominion upon an earth saturated with the blood of the saints. But at that moment – or so we may assume – God's judgment suddenly descends. The angels of judgment step forward. The Third World War – a nuclear war – breaks out. Everyone is seized by horror and terror. The heavens rain fire and brimstone. And like a hammock the earth is swung to and fro. It totters and sways, the atmosphere pervaded with poison gases.

The group of royal priests, the bridal souls, who were protected during the persecution, tremble, pray and trust God. Having been destined for the rapture, they will also be protected from the wrath of the mighty God, which will descend upon the godless in order to purge them from the earth. The bridal souls, who together with other righteous souls will be numbered among the survivors, must then live on a wholly devastated, gruesome earth covered with innumerable corpses. With this God has prepared a further period of suffering for them. After the terrible days of persecution and the horrors of the nuclear war, His elect must live on this ravaged earth among despairing people.

But at the same time they have a tremendous commission – to call the new generation to Jesus. For after the Third World War and all the shattering experiences a new generation will arise that is open to the things of God. There will probably be a brief but fruitful period of evangelism when much will be achieved for the Lord. Suffering will have prepared the ground for revivals of greater spiritual depth than ever before. And during this period a number of souls will be added to the bridal host.

God has a marvellous purpose for the group that He has chosen for the rapture and protected during the afflictions. In the years when sin and the power of evil prevailed, these souls humbled themselves – not only beneath their own sins, but beneath the abominable sins and blasphemies in the world. They wept with their Lord over all that the godless and the apostate had inflicted upon Him. These bridal souls lived for the sole purpose of showing Him their love, of comforting and consoling Him in His deep anguish. They suffered with Him, praying fervently that men would repent, and they themselves repented. Now in addition to the immense sufferings they had undergone during the persecution and worldwide disaster, God wants to use the suffering of the following period up to and including the beginning of the Antichrist's reign, which will bring new persecution, to further prepare the elect for the rapture. To attain this tremendous goal, which God has in mind for them, the suffering could not be any less.

They are souls marked by the cross. Their lives abound with suffering; indeed, they are saturated with suffering. But in the same measure that they must suffer, they are transformed by Jesus into His image and wholly sanctified. These bridal souls have been chosen by God to be caught up in the clouds to meet the Lord while they are still alive – a privilege never granted to any other group of believers – and they will behold Him whom none can behold without holiness. This explains why God must place them in the crucible of purification. But in the twinkling of an eye everything will be changed. Suddenly, at midnight, when the Antichrist is about to display his full power, the cry of the archangel will resound and the trumpet of God will be blown. The Lord Himself will descend from heaven, and these souls, who have been prepared and sanctified, will be caught up to meet Him in the air, clothed with glory and immortality (1 Thessalonians 4:16 f.). What a moment that will be! These believers will experience an ascension similar to their Lord's. They will ascend directly to Jesus without tasting death. And from this moment on they will be united with the Lord for ever.

A momentous event for the whole of heaven! We can imagine all the angelic hosts, princely figures endowed with the glory of God, forming a guard of honour for the royal wedding procession of Jesus and the bridal host, the bride of the Lamb. What songs of rejoicing the angelic choirs will raise as the bridal host is received by Jesus and escorted into the golden city! Ineffable joy will seize the souls who have been caught up to the Lord. Delivered from a dreadful, evil and hell-like earth and transferred in the twinkling of an eye into Jesus' kingdom of light and joy! Who can comprehend what this means! Now they may behold Jesus after having clung to Him in blind faith during the time of great affliction. Their joy is beyond all compare. They are united with people from all ages who partook of the first resurrection and with whom they now form the bride of the Lamb. Having prepared herself, the bride is attired in shining white linen and may go in to celebrate the Marriage Feast of the Lamb.

Angel choirs with joy are singing,
"Hark! the Bridegroom comes!"

All the heav'nly spheres are ringing
With the cry, "The Bridegroom comes!"
And the bride with bliss is trembling,
For the wedding is at hand.
O the wondrous joy and glory —
Marriage Supper of the Lamb!

Jesus, the belovèd Saviour,
Comes in majesty.
Angel hosts their praises render,
Worshipping their Lord and King.
But His heart is yearning only
For His bride in fervent love.
After waiting, watching, suff'ring,
She is wed to Him above.

Now her heart with joy is bursting.
Christ, her Lord, has come.
Filled with praise, she sings rejoicing,
"Glory, glory to the Lamb."
Heav'n resounds with exultation;
Joy o'er all things reigns supreme.
Grief is changed to jubilation;
Glory came from suffering.*

The Marriage Feast of the Lamb commences. The last
martyrs of the Antichrist's reign have been added to the
bridal host; the purposes of God have been brought to
consummation. During the wedding celebrations in
heaven, the millennial kingdom marks the beginning of
the Kingdom of God on earth. But later, after the Last
Judgment, the dominion of God is fully manifested on
the new earth. The new heaven and the new earth have

* See *The King Draws Near* (songs about Jesus' second coming and the
heavenly glory).

become a reality in fulfilment of His promise, "Behold, I make all things new."

Now Jesus reigns together with the company of kings and priests, His bride, without whom He does nothing (Revelation 2:26). Indeed, He even shares the throne with her (Revelation 3:21). He dwells with her in that city which is the centre of the new earth. Thus the City of God is comprised of these priests and kings, the bride of the Lamb, whose number was completed in our times with souls who were called to be martyrs and others who were protected for the rapture. At last, the marvellous plans of God have been brought to consummation. The divine purposes contained in the sealed scroll, which only the slain Lamb was entitled to open, by virtue of His sacrificial death, have now been fulfilled after God, in His humble patience, had sought for thousands of years to bring mankind back to Himself. A song of rejoicing is raised by the bride as she worships the Lamb, who gained the victory over Satan and sin and who created a new heaven and a new earth by His blood.

Then I saw a new heaven and a new earth; for the first heaven and the first earth had passed away, and the sea was no more. And I saw the holy city, new Jerusalem, coming down out of heaven from God, prepared as a bride adorned for her husband; and I heard a great voice from the throne saying, "Behold, the dwelling of God is with men. He will dwell with them, and they shall be his people, and God himself will be with them; he will wipe away every tear from their eyes, and death shall be no more, neither shall there be mourning nor crying nor pain any more, for the former things have passed away."

And he who sat upon the throne said, "Behold, I make all things new." Also he said, "Write this, for these words are trustworthy and true."   Revelation 21:1-5

"Yes, I am coming soon!" "Amen. Come, Lord Jesus!" With these words the Book of Revelation closes, and thus they are of the utmost significance. The believers, especially in the Early Church, used to greet each other with these words. But it was more than a form of greeting. It was a promise that they held up against all the satanic onslaughts and against all the persecution and affliction that they had to live through. Like a bright star illumining the night, these words of Jesus, "I am coming soon!" imparted hope to them. And how often the cry, "Come soon, Lord Jesus! Come soon!" was raised to heaven in reply — especially by the persecuted and sorely afflicted!

Yes, Jesus is coming again soon! This fact instils a courageous faith in us too, the believers of today, who are harassed and persecuted by Satan in a world that is increasingly coming under his dominion. Jesus is coming. He is coming as the Last, the End of all — just as He testifies in the closing verses of Revelation, "I am the Alpha and the Omega, the first and the last, the beginning and the end" (Revelation 22:13). With this, the Lord gives us a promise so tremendous that it causes all the terrors of the end times to fade away, as if they were swallowed up by an abyss. These words, which so to speak mark the end of all of Satan's activities, his domination and victorious might on earth in the end times, are a royal declaration. In more than one place in Revelation, Jesus says of Himself, "I am the first and the last!" He is the First, by whom all things were made (Hebrews 1:2). He existed before all things, also before the creation of Lucifer, who fell away from God and became Jesus' adversary, Satan. And as the glorified Lamb, Jesus will be the Last, that is, the final Victor.

In the end times, however, it appears more and more as though Satan, and not Jesus, is "the last", the victor, who will take everything into his hands, establish his rule and in the end create a new world. But one statement stands immovable like solid rock. No one can obliterate it. Figuratively speaking, it has been written in blood, for the One who uttered it paid the price with His life-blood. It is the words of Jesus, "I am the Last!" Jesus will return as the Last, as the End, for with His coming an end will be put to Satan's power and Satan himself. It will happen overnight. Suddenly Jesus will appear. And Satan, who posed as "the last", will be condemned to the bottomless pit and his kingdom will be destroyed. His power and dominion will be over for ever. This will be the final outcome.

With His words "I am the Last", it seems as though Jesus is invalidating with a single stroke of the pen the innumerable speeches and writings that are directed against Him today. Influential people on the political and religious scene and international, anti-Christian organizations appear to govern the world more and more with each new day by the opinions they put forth. They can say and write whatever they please, yes, exert control over everything and even kill Jesus' followers – but Jesus, and not they, will remain the First and the Last, even if they proclaim their supremacy a thousand times over. For it is not Satan and those who belong to him – the Antichrist and his predecessors – who created the world as "the first". This Jesus did, in unity with the Father, and it was He who shed His precious blood as the innocent Lamb for the redemption and renewal of the world. Satan and his vassals are but created beings; moreover, they stand under the curse of sin. Consequently, they have no power whatsoever to speak the last word to mankind and to establish the final dominion. How ludicrous is such an endeavour! It is merely a utopian scheme, born out of megalomania and hatred of God – a hatred that destroys itself by its very frenzy. Therefore, all their plans too will end in destruction.

Jesus Christ alone is Lord; He is the Lord of lords. When He declares that a kingdom will come, it will come beyond all shadow of doubt. He already proved Himself to be Lord at the beginning when the world was created through Him, and thus He demonstrated that He is the First. And since Jesus Christ "is the same yesterday and today and for ever", He will also be the Last, who alone will emerge as Victor and remain when all else has fallen. Never shall we be able to thank Jesus enough for giving us His royal promise, "I am coming. I am the First and the Last and the Living One, the Beginning and the End!"

Indeed, He is coming as the Last, as the End of all. How much these words mean to us all, who have to live in the pre-antichristian era! It is as if God has given us a pledge – a pledge that can transform every situation of distress, because it contains the solution. The powers of darkness and the servants of Satan think that they can torment Jesus' followers at will with their ideologies, which give rise to the misery of sin, to crime, violence, Satanism, outrageous blasphemy and the persecution of God's own. However, they are forced to leave the world stage when Jesus comes. Satan together with his adherents, the Satanists and the instruments of the Antichrist, will disappear, never to be seen again. They will be banished by Jesus to the bottomless pit and later to the lake of fire (Revelation 20:10). The final Victor in this terrible epoch will be Jesus, whom man has once again condemned to death today and, so to speak, buried beneath the earth. He stands arrayed in majesty and power and declares, "I am the Last." Indeed, He is the Last, the End of all, who will remain when all else has fallen, and His dominion will also remain, for it is an *everlasting* dominion (Daniel 7:14).

The Prophet Daniel saw that the Lord gave the beast permission to wage war against the saints and prevail over them only "until the coming of the one of great age who gave judgement in favour of the saints of the Most High, when the time came for the saints to take over the kingdom" (Daniel 7:22 *The Jerusalem Bible*). Then the beast's "dominion shall be taken away, to be consumed and destroyed to the end. And the kingdom and the dominion and the greatness of the kingdoms under the whole heaven shall be given to the people of the saints of the Most High; their kingdom shall be an everlasting kingdom, and all dominions shall serve and obey them" (Daniel 7:26 f.).

"Our Lord and King will come as the Last, the final Victor." What a triumphant declaration for His own! With it they can rout the enemy. The Lord will establish His everlasting kingdom, which will embrace all the peoples of the world and be succeeded by none.

This assurance has the power to dispel all fears, as I personally experienced. During the Third Reich in Germany I was once summoned to appear before the secret police and interrogated for several hours. Humanly speaking, there was no hope of my release, but nevertheless I was filled with a royal assurance of victory and could not do otherwise than testify to the officials cross-examining me, "But this Jesus will come again and establish His kingdom, His everlasting kingdom..." This was the triumphant certainty that filled me and it was greater than all fear and sense of caution. The dictator, during whose regime I was subjected to cross-examination, was but a predecessor of the beast. At first he too was always victorious and referred to his kingdom, the Third Reich, as an everlasting kingdom. However, it was short-lived and ended in total defeat. How much more will the triumphant conviction that Jesus' kingdom is of eternal duration and that He is the Last, the End of all, carry His own through in the end times, during the reign of pre-antichristian despots and later of the beast himself!

This knowledge is a source of triumph for all those who belong to the army of the Lamb. They have a hope that will not be disappointed, for the promises of their Lord are trustworthy. He is the Truth. Up till now every prophecy has come true, and thus the prophecies concerning the end times will also come true. At the close of the age the beast will rise to power and mercilessly persecute and terrorize the Christians – but only to meet his final defeat when he and his kingdom will be overthrown for ever.

"Yes, I am coming. I am coming as the Last, the End of all." This promise of Jesus is invisibly written above each chapter in Revelation that depicts the horrors and terrors of the antichristian dominion and the forces of Satan. Words are insufficient to describe Jesus' royal splendour and power. "King of kings" – this title of Jesus Christ is written in eternal letters above the reality of this age when, as God's own, we are still experiencing the great might of Satan.

Despite all the defeats the kingdom of Jesus seems to suffer in the pre-antichristian and antichristian era, His own know from the very outset that the victory of Jesus is certain. For He and His kingdom bear within them the divine law that death is followed by resurrection. His kingdom is built on a foundation of wounds and outpoured blood. As Jesus hung on the cross, His commission seemed to lie in ruins. Everything, including our Lord Himself, was doomed to death, destroyed. But this alone gave rise to His victory. And the same principle will hold true in the antichristian era when Jesus will seem to suffer His greatest defeat. His name is

"Omega". He will emerge from the battle as the final Victor, the triumphant Lamb, who crushed the serpent under His feet, and as the Lord of lords, to whom all power has been given in heaven and on earth. Jesus is Victor. He is coming soon!

But why did Jesus give His own the wonderful promise contained in the little word "soon" if His everlasting rule over all the kingdoms of the world would not be established until a long period of maturing had elapsed? Have not believers for almost 2,000 years waited in vain for the fulfilment of this promise? Jesus had a wise purpose. With this word "soon" He wished to produce something special in His own, something that we would prize for all eternity – a deep yearning and a sense of expectancy and at the same time patient endurance, for the latter in particular will bring us a crown. In heaven we shall then give God thanks for this crown and worship Him for His ways, which are true and just.

Paul, and above all John, the favourite disciple of Jesus, attained the crown of patient endurance. With great yearning they looked forward to Jesus' return, expecting it to come very soon. But Paul suffered martyrdom without ever seeing that day. And John had to remain on earth for scores of years, reaching the advanced age of about a hundred, suffering ever anew the disappointment of not seeing his hopes materialize. Jesus did not come. But what did this disappointment in the word "soon" create in him? Patient endurance. This attribute is especially important for everyone who must live in an age of martyrdom. And our generation is approaching a worldwide persecution of Christians under an antichristian dominion. How fervent will the cry be then, "Come soon, Lord Jesus!" "Here is a call for the endurance of the saints" (Revelation 14:12) – how meaningful these words of Jesus are to His own when they are persecuted, hated, ostracized, arrested, tortured and killed! In this age of persecution and affliction the call to patient endurance applies to His own more than ever, because Jesus seems to conceal Himself and does not appear. It seems as if He is no longer to be found anywhere. He will doubtlessly come one day, but He has not come "soon." When will He come?

"Shall we ever experience His return?" large numbers of tortured souls may sigh. Even now in many countries the persecuted, whose number increases from year to year, wait yearningly for Jesus to come and set up His kingdom and deliver them from the power and hatred of anti-Christian people. In this situation it is as if Jesus were saying, "I am coming. My word is true. However, the day and hour is known to none but the Father. Your sole concern now must be to endure in patience, to remain steadfast and faithful when the diabolical torture and all the suffering seem almost unbearable to you. All who suffer patiently and wait steadfastly will experience that I come to them even now, and above they will reign with Me, that is, they will be kings and wear crowns. Persevere. I shall come at the right moment. When the suffering seems too hard for you to bear, I shall come to you."

However, it is not only a question of endurance. As Revelation challenges us, it is equally important that we remain loyal to Jesus and keep faith (Revelation 14:12). Jesus would perhaps go on to say, "Whoever believes in Me believes in My love. And My love can never forsake you. It will come when the night is at its darkest. 'I shall come to you' was My promise long ago to My troubled disciples, and I came to them when they were in deep distress after My crucifixion — fearful, persecuted, disappointed and in despair. I am called Faithful and True. This will be My name when I come again to execute judgment upon the world — and I am coming, also to vindicate you and to punish the world for the way you were treated. Yes, I am coming, but not alone; for as I said, 'I am coming soon, and my reward is with me, to repay everyone according to the deeds he has done' (Revelation 22:12 *The Living Bible*). And what did you do? You suffered. Suffering brings the greatest glory and the greatest reward. I shall give you My reward when I come to My own – either when I call them home individually or when I gather the bridal souls at the rapture. The reward I give will be great, for 'patient endurance' means that you have made innumerable acts of dedication to suffering. And even if the Bridegroom tarries, wait for Him. I am coming. I am coming surely, but at a moment when you least expect it, that is, when the earth is at its darkest. Then the words will come true:

'I AM THE FIRST AND THE LAST.
I AM COMING. I HAVE COME.' "

Supplementary Reading by Basilea Schlink

1. leaflets

    Jesus Mocked Today (an answer to "Jesus Christ Superstar")

    ...but at whose expense? (an answer to "Godspell" — British edition)

    Jesus Blasphemed Again (an answer to "Godspell" — American edition)

2. Never Before in the History of the Church 32 pp.

3. If I Only Love Jesus 24 pp.

4. You Will Never Be the Same 192 pp.

5. Let Me Stand at Your Side 160 pp.

6. Repentance — The Joy-filled Life 62 pp.

7. My All for Him 160 pp.

8. What Comes after Death? — The Reality of Heaven and Hell 128 pp.

9. Pollution — But There *Is* an Answer 64 pp.
    (A Matter of Life and Death — American edition)

10. Countdown to World Disaster — Hope and Protection for the Future 96 pp.

11. Hope for Man in a Hopeless World (American edition) 122 pp.

12. Escaping the Web of Deception 64 pp.

13. The Eve of Persecution 90 pp.

A Foretaste of Heaven 416 pp. Illustrated, full-length autobiography (I Found the Key to the Heart of God – American edition)